MAMA'S COOKING

Celebrities Remember Mama's Best Recipe

Esther Blumenfeld and Lynne Alpern

Peachtree Publishers, Ltd.

Published by
Peachtree Publishers, Ltd.
494 Armour Circle, N.E.
Atlanta, Georgia 30324

Manufactured in the United States of America

10 9 8 7 6 5 4 3 2 1

Library of Congress Catalog Card Number 88-60004

ISBN 0-934601-48-8

Cover design and illustration by Paulette L. Lambert

TABLE OF CONTENTS

I.   OF CHUCKLES AND CHUCK ROAST (Introduction) 1

II. WARM-UP ACTS (Appetizers, Soups, & Salads) 5
     Theodore Bikel — Authentic Chopped Liver 7
     Johnny Rutherford — Doris Rutherford's Pimento Cheese 9
     Peter Nero — Borekas de Queso (Cheese Turnovers) 11
     Michael S. Dukakis — Spinach Pie (Spanakopita) 14
     Edward Kennedy — Cape Cod Fish Chowder 16
     Louie Anderson — Cream of Broccoli Soup 18
     Leo Buscaglia — Minestrone Soup 20
     Jean Kasem — Vegetable Soup 22
     Barbara Bush — All-American Clam Chowder..................... 24
     Lee Iacocca — Antoinette Iacocca's Italian Meatball Soup 25
     Esther Blumenfeld — Ruth Richter's Easy & Delicious Chicken Soup.. 27
     Christo — Tarator (Summer Soup) 29
     Jimmy Carter — Lime Congealed Salad 31
     Jane Alexander — Cucumber & Onion Salad 33
     Richard G. Lugar — Lugar's Pasta Salad 35
     Paul Anka — Taboulay (Parsley Salad) 37
     Ana-Alicia — Chinese Chicken Salad 39

III. HEADLINERS (Main Dishes) 41
     Monty Hall — Sweet and Sour Stewed Tongue 43
     Dee Wallace Stone — Brisket 45
     Lewis Grizzard — Country Fried Steak 47

Edward I. Koch — Hamburgers 49
Mary Kay Ash — Chicken and Dumplings 50
Norman Vincent Peale — Chicken Fricassee 52
Gene Cernan — Chicken Spaghetti 54
Geraldine A. Ferraro — Manicotti Pancakes 56
Pat Boone — Chili-Mac from the Boone Kitchen 59
Irving Wallace — Hamburger Pudding à la I.W. 61
Bob Griese — Ida Griese's Chili 63
Joe Montana — Montana Ravioli 65
Ted Stevens — Ann Stevens's Dishwasher Fish 67
Clint Eastwood — Spaghetti Western 69
Jake Steinfeld — Shrimp Parmigiana 72
Mary Healy — Shrimp Creole 75
Debbie Reynolds — Taco Pie 77
Richard Gephardt — Filet of Sole 80
Vince Dooley — Crab Omelet Sandwich 82
George Deukmejian — Crab Fiesta Bake 85

IV.   SECOND BANANAS (Side Dishes) 87
Benjamin Spock — Oatmeal 89
Bill Anderson — Cheese Soufflé and Cornmeal Pancakes 90
Judy Woodruff — Anna Lee Woodruff's Refrigerator Rolls 92
Hoyt Axton — Jalapeño Cornbread and Granny's Butter Rolls 95
Judith Ivey — Orange Date Bread 97
Erskine Caldwell — Homestead Black-Eyed Peas
    and Mother's Cornbread 99
Mario M. Cuomo — Polenta 101
Avner Eisenberg — Lokshen Kugel 103
DeForest Kelley — Company Grits 105
Alex Haley — Fried Corn 107

V. ENCORES (Desserts) 109
    Lynne Alpern — Ruth Shapiro's Lusty Cheesecake 110
    Willard Scott — Brown Sugar Pound Cake 113
    Jeff Van Note — Sheath Cake 115
    Christopher Parkening—Jessie Lee Marshall's Buttermilk Coffeecake . . 117
    Joseph Paterno — Paterno Orange Cake 119
    Ed McMahon — Radio Doughnuts 121
    Bob Dole — Seven-Layer Cookies 123
    Wally Amos — Famous Amos' Raisin-Filled Chocolate Chip Cookies . . 125
    Meredith MacRae — Crème Brulée 127
    Orrin G. Hatch — Chipped Chocolate Pie 129
    Porter Wagoner — Porter Wagoner Fudge 130
    Laurence J. Peter — Savory Rice Pudding 132
    Nancy Wilson — Trifle 134
    Betty Talmadge — Charlotte Russe 135
    Cathy Lee Crosby — Persimmon Pudding 137

VI. CRITICS' CORNER 139
    Douglas Fairbanks, Jr. 141
    Helen Gurley Brown 142
    Jake's Fish à la Veracruzana 144
    Chicken with Sherry Wine Sauce 148
    Chinese Pepper Steak 150
    Moroccan Lamb 152
    Green Pepper and Tomato Salad and Orange Slices 153

DEDICATION

For four celebrated men in my life —
   My husband, Warren, whose good heart and strong shoulders carried me when my leg couldn't;
   My son, Josh, who paid me back in kind for twenty years of love, caring and TV dinners;
   My big brother, David, who can always make me laugh, and
   My father, Karl, who taught me about faith, courage and the value of each day. With love and gratitude —

Esther

To three world-class food lovers —
      An A-1 dad, Julian;
      A nonpareil brother, Doug;
      And a matchless husband, Bob —
   The best audience a leg of lamb ever had.

Lynne

I

OF CHUCKLES AND CHUCK ROAST

(An Introduction)

Never make friends with novelists because, like Emily Ellison, they are always full of irresistible ideas. So when she suggested we do a book of celebrities' favorite recipes and stories from their mothers, Emily was then free to return to her word processor to create beautiful images while we were left captivated by an idea and, like Blanche DuBois, "dependent on the kindness of strangers."

Compared to us, Tennessee Williams' Blanche had it easy. At least those "strangers" were her own sister and brother-in-law (even if he was a bit untidy), while we could only sit and wait for some of the most famous people in the world to respond to our letters. Our editor kept encouraging us. But how much can you believe from a man who, once a month when the moon is full, is unchained from his desk so he can sharpen his eyeteeth on manuscripts?

But this is America, where everything is possible. And where people are *what* they are, not because of royal lineage, but because of their talent and accomplishments . . . and what their mothers fed them.

Happily, the better-fed celebrities responded. Thanks to them, you will find between these covers the favorite specialties of their moms (plus a few from wives as well).

But fixing Mary Kay Ash's "Chicken and Dumplings" or Ed McMahon's "Radio Doughnuts" is only half the fun. For while "Sweet and Sour Tongue" may be Monty Hall's favorite childhood dish, cooking is the universal "mother tongue" through which Mama's nurturing is translated into a feast of love . . . occasionally punctuated, of course, by gastronomic gaffs and culinary capers. Like the encounter between Lynne's seventy-three-year-old mother, her justifiably-hankered-for scrumptious cheesecake and twenty-three lusty Texans in a topless bar.

Thus you will find in these pages not only the recipes themselves but also funny and touching anecdotes, as our celebrities take out treasured stories fragrant with memories and let them cool on our windowsill for all to see.

For this we thank them, one and all.

For this we thank our own mothers, Ruth May Richter and Ruth Miller Shapiro, for always smiling when we share their funny stories that keep bubbling to the surface. It's hard to keep a good laugh down.

For this you will be filled with laughter, joy and some delicious concoctions. And who knows? Maybe, if you can get your children to eat Benjamin Spock's "Oatmeal" and DeForest Kelley's "Company Grits," they too will grow up to be famous doctors.

So read on, enjoy and dream.

II

WARM-UP ACTS

(Appetizers, Soups, and Salads)

My mother-in-law's cooking motto is, "If you're out of it, improvise." I had always assumed she meant a minor ingredient — until I became the mother of an infant son who vocally encouraged family get-togethers at two o'clock every morning.

"Out of it" described both my kitchen cabinets and the state I was in when my husband, Warren, called one afternoon and announced he was bringing home an out-of-town client for a quick drink and snack before driving him to the airport.

With "don't fuss" ringing in my ears, I hung up the phone and began frantically searching through my refrigerator and cabinets. Except for a box of Melba toast, there was no adult food anywhere in our apartment.

Later, raving about my hors d'oeuvres, our guest begged me to send his wife the recipe for what I had announced as "G & G Paté," which I had brushed with butter, broiled and served on Melba toast.

After he left, Warren marveled at my lightning-quick creativity. Smacking his lips, he asked, "That hors d'oeuvre tasted kind of familiar, but I couldn't quite place it. What's in 'G & G Paté' anyway?"

"Garlic and Gerber's Pureed Veal," I smirked, "and I'm not sharing *that* recipe with anyone."

—EB

THEODORE BIKEL

Actor, singer

Mother: Miriam (Riegler) Bikel

My mother's strongest suit was not her cooking, though personally I never minded it very much. That may be because I knew very little else until I left home and discovered the haute cuisine of the world's chefs.

I recall once, at Passover time, when Mother made matzoh balls. Dad remarked, "The other day, one of these matzoh balls slipped and fell on the tiled floor; look at the tile — it cracked!"

If I had a favorite dish, it was Mama's chopped liver. The recipe was actually my grandmother's — *her* cooking, I remember, was somewhat more flavorful although of the same variety: Eastern European Jewish and less than strictly kosher. As to the chopped liver, it was much spicier than the varieties served in delicatessens. The texture was also grainier; hand-chopped ingredients and hand-mixed preparation are far preferable to the blender method.

—Theodore Bikel

AUTHENTIC CHOPPED LIVER

1/3 cup rendered chicken fat,
 enough to coat pan
2 medium onions
1 cup chicken livers

pinch sugar
1 1/2 pinch salt
3 hard-boiled eggs
salt and pepper

Fry the onions, chicken livers, sugar and salt in chicken fat until liver is no longer pink inside. Hand chop liver and onions together with eggs. Add salt and pepper to taste, and a drop of hot water. Put in mold and refrigerate.

Twice a week without fail Simon's mother made fresh soup from scratch — beef on Monday and chicken every Friday. Growing up in the Depression, her frugal ways were deeply ingrained. Thus she always added the odds-and-ends leftovers of the previous three days. Her children teased her constantly about the wide-ranging contents.

One Friday evening, as his mama ladled up dinner as usual, Simon found yet another ingredient added to his favorite chicken soup. There, right in the middle of the sliced carrots, diced celery, and leftover potato chunks, floated a shiny, Barbie-sized kitchen sink. He never complained again.

—LA

JOHNNY RUTHERFORD

Professional race car driver

Mother: Doris Rutherford

Our whole family has a *big* favorite — pimento cheese to make sandwiches and also for stuffing celery. Ha! In our family you are not considered a *real* Rutherford if you don't like pimento cheese.

—Johnny Rutherford

DORIS RUTHERFORD'S PIMENTO CHEESE

1 lb. Cheddar cheese
1 lb. sharp Cheddar cheese
1 large jar chopped pimentos,
   with juice

2 tbl. grated onion
mayonnaise
salt and pepper to taste

The cheeses should be put through a food grinder (you may add the onion also instead of grating it). Then add pimentoes, salt, pepper and enough mayonnaise to make it easily spreadable.

☆　　☆　　☆

My brother, Doug, a marine biologist at the University of Puerto Rico in Mayaguez, has always been an adventurous eater. Over the years he's learned to curb his appetite but never his curiosity.

One night, invited to a colleague's home for a party, Doug arrived early. Sally and Mark ushered him in, then retreated to the kitchen for last-minute preparations. Left unattended, Doug wandered around and browsed through a bookshelf until a plate of neatly arranged concentric circles of hors d'oeuvres commanded his attention.

Looking over the selection, he recognized all the appetizers except the center one: a Ritz cracker smothered with cream cheese and topped with an incredibly beautiful one-inch, pale blue fish — whole. Not wanting to miss the opportunity of savoring this morsel, he popped it into his mouth just as his hostess returned.

"What was that unusual tasting fish I just tried?" Doug quizzed.

"You mean you ate that one in the center?" gasped Sally. "Mark found that one floating on top of our tank this morning. You just swallowed his warped sense of humor!"

—LA

10

PETER NERO

Pianist, conductor, composer, arranger

Mother: Mary (Menasche) Nierow

Borekas are a middle-Eastern delicacy, originating in Turkey. Although my mother was born in the USA, her mother and forebears emanated from the island of Rhodes, in the Mediterranean. Over the centuries, Rhodes was alternately governed by Turkey and Greece, so the cuisine is a mixture of both ethnic cultures.

My mother's family is Sephardic and traces its roots back to Spain in the fifteenth century. Their cuisine, referred to as "Ladino," is a combination of the above and that of Spain. Therefore, my early life's gastronomical sustenance consisted of traditional Jewish-American cooking (my father came to the U.S. at age thirteen from Russia) and "Ladino." It was a great childhood and I enjoyed being overweight.

At that time, it was usually my grandmother and aunts who commanded the kitchens and, as a result, the matriarchs cooked for family get-togethers. Now that

11

most of them have passed on, my mother has taken up the banner, and in grand style indeed.

In September of 1987 we celebrated Mom's seventy-fifth birthday at the home of my brother and his family. Now the matriarch, she enlisted the help of my father (who last year celebrated his seventy-fifth birthday) and made *her* version of borekas. I am happy to say that not only has the tradition been passed down gloriously, it has been improved.

Mom made enough extras so that we could return home and have enough to last us for a week. I finished them in two days. Goodbye diet, hello borekas.

—Peter Nero

BOREKAS de QUESO (Cheese Turnovers)

MASA (dough)

1 cup oil	1/2 tsp. salt
1 cup cold water	5 cups flour (unsifted)

Preheat oven to 375.

Blend thoroughly oil, water and salt. Add flour all at once. Blend thoroughly. Break off portions the size of a large walnut and roll on slightly floured board into rounds 3-4″ in diameter and approximately 1/8″ thick. Fill with 1 tbl. cheese filling and lap pastry over like a turnover. Seal edges of dough so that filling will not run out during baking. Bake in a dry non-stick pan in 375 oven for about 45 minutes, or until light golden brown. Best when served hot. May be frozen if desired. Husbands can be *very* helpful in rolling out the dough.

GOMO de QUESO (cheese filling)

2 pkg. farmer's cheese
½ lb. feta cheese, crumbled
3 eggs, slightly beaten

¼ cup grated Parmesan cheese
¼ cup grated Romano cheese
¼ cup matzoh meal (to thicken)

Mix together cheese, eggs and matzoh meal. Mixture should have consistency of thick but fluffy filling. Fill and seal as directed in the Masa recipe. Brush tops of Borekas with beaten egg and sprinkle with sesame seeds or grated cheese before baking. Bake as directed.

Variations of fillings

Instead of farmer's cheese, substitute:
1 lb. ricotta cheese *or*
1 lb. of boiled and mashed potatoes *or*
1 cup well-cooked rice *or*
1 lb. lean ground beef simmered with onions, pepper, lemon juice *or*
2 bunches fresh spinach, washed, dried and finely chopped *or*
2 eggplants, sautéed with onions and 1 can solid pack tomatoes.

Mesas Alegres!

MICHAEL S. DUKAKIS

Governor of Massachusetts

Mother: Euterpe (Boukis) Dukakis

Michael always was helpful around the kitchen, but his own cooking skills are relatively new. He has asked me for advice and recipes over the years.

However, when he was younger, he did do camp cooking with the Boy Scouts. I remember once when he was about fourteen or so, he was preparing for a camping weekend. He had bought hamburger and rolls for the expedition and was home, ready to divide the meat for patties. He had bought two pounds of hamburger.

I remember asking him, "How many hamburgers do you plan to make out of that two pounds?" And Michael, who has a reputation for being thrifty, looked at me with a twinkle in his eyes and said, "Oh, about one hundred."

—Euterpe Dukakis

SPINACH PIE (SPANAKOPITA)

1 box fillo (also known as
    phyllo, or strudel dough)
2 sticks melted butter
3 pkg. frozen *leaf* spinach
1 small onion, minced, or 3
    scallions cut in 1″ pieces

2 tbl. olive or salad oil
1/2 tsp. salt, a little pepper
3/4 lb. feta cheese, well crumbled
    a little dill, fresh preferably
4 eggs

Put frozen spinach in refrigerator before going to bed. In the morning cut it in 1/2″ slices both ways. Spread out on a large pan 'til thoroughly thawed. Squeeze between hands until all liquid is removed.

Preheat oven to 375. Sauté onion or scallions in oil 4-5 minutes. Add onion mixture to well-beaten eggs. Add dill, seasoning, finely crumbled cheese and the spinach. Stir well to mix thoroughly.

In a 9″ x 12″ pan which has been well oiled or buttered, spread six layers of the fillo, each layer lightly brushed with butter (follow directions for use on box). Spread the filling evenly. Cover with six more sheets of fillo, each layer brushed with butter, top layer brushed generously. Fold the edges neatly and butter well.

Bake 50-60 minutes. Let cool thoroughly before cutting in serving pieces. I cut mine in 2″ squares. Serve hot. The cut-up pieces can be lined up in a box and frozen. To serve, thaw thoroughly and bake again 'til sizzling (don't brown too much).

Caution: If you have never used fillo before, ask a friend who knows. It can be tricky. Any fillo left over can be wrapped well (the way it came) with a damp towel and put in the refrigerator for a few days, or refrozen. This can also be served as a side dish. Makes 24 squares.

EDWARD KENNEDY

U.S. Senator from Massachusetts

Mother: Rose (Fitzgerald) Kennedy

We can assure you that the following delectable dish, from Ted Kennedy, has not been allowed near any marine biologists of our acquaintance. . . .

SENATOR KENNEDY'S CAPE COD FISH CHOWDER

2 lbs. fresh haddock
2 oz. salt pork, diced
2 medium onions, sliced
1 cup chopped celery
4 large potatoes, diced

1 bay leaf, crumbled
4 cups milk
2 tbl. butter or margarine
1 tsp. salt
freshly ground pepper to taste

Simmer haddock in 2 cups of water for 15 minutes. Drain fish and reserve the broth. Remove the skin and bones from the fish. Sauté the diced salt pork in a large pot until crisp. Remove salt pork and sauté the onions in the pork fat until golden brown.

Add fish, celery, potatoes and bay leaf. Measure reserved fish broth, plus enough boiling water, to make 3 cups liquid. Add to pot and simmer 30 minutes. Add milk and butter and simmer for an additional 5 minutes, or until well heated. Season with salt and pepper. Makes 8 servings.

LOUIE ANDERSON

Comedian

Mother: Ora Zella Anderson

With five girls and six boys in my house, I spent a lot of time in the kitchen. I was always making their favorites — corn chowder, cream puffs with vanilla filling, meatloaf and cream of broccoli soup. I still make them, but now I use a lot of shortcuts, like substituting frozen chopped broccoli for fresh broccoli in my soup. These days we all want to live fast.

Back then I'd make two chocolate cakes per meal, and there still weren't any leftovers. With eleven children, some are always dropping in, so I'm always "cooking heavy!"

—Ora Anderson

CREAM OF BROCCOLI SOUP

1 small onion, thinly sliced
1 leek, thinly sliced (white part only)
1 small rib celery, sliced (without leaves)
1 tbl. butter
1/2 cup water
2 10-oz. pkg. frozen chopped broccoli
2 tsp. salt
dash cayenne pepper
2 tbl. uncooked rice
2 cups chicken broth
1/2 cup cream or milk

Put onion, leek, celery, butter and water in 2-qt. saucepan; simmer slowly 2 minutes over medium heat. In separate saucepan cook broccoli until tender and drain (reserve 1/2 cup liquid).

Add salt, cayenne, rice and 1 cup broth to onion mixture in saucepan; simmer 15 minutes. Do not boil. Pour mixture into blender; cover and run on high until liquified. Pour back into saucepan.

Put broccoli and remaining chicken broth in blender; cover and run on high until broccoli is liquified. If mixture becomes too thick to flow, add reserved broccoli cooking liquid to thin. Add broccoli to onion mixture in saucepan; add cream. Heat (do not boil) and serve.

LEO BUSCAGLIA

Educator, lecturer, author

Mother: Rosa (Cagna) Buscaglia

There are so many things in life which link me to my past, but few have been more lasting than Mama's soup. For my family, it became an economic indicator more accurate than Wall Street. We could always judge our financial condition by the thickness of the soup. A thick brew indicated that things were going well with the Buscaglias; a watery soup denoted meager, less plentiful times. No matter the abundance of food served in our home, nothing was ever thrown out. Everything ended up in the soup pot.

Minestrone was medicinal. It served both physical and mental needs. If we got hurt, Mama's remedy was always a Band-Aid, a hug and a bowl of soup. It cured colds, fever, headaches, indigestion, heartaches and loneliness.

How often a bowl of minestrone served to unite us and bring us together in warmth and joy! It was an act of communion. When people dropped in, strangers included, we would soon find ourselves huddled around the kitchen table, talking over a bowl of steaming soup. It took care of breakfast, a quick lunch or a midnight snack. It was sometimes even a sign that someone needed to talk.

Mama died about ten years ago, six years before Papa. Somehow, the house was never the same. Someone turned the gas off under the minestrone pot the day after she was buried, and a whole era went out with the flame.

There are so few things that one can really count on these days. We need more minestrone pots in the world. I long for the security, the aroma, the taste. I'm sure there are still such soups simmering in houses all over the world. Long may they simmer!

—**Leo Buscaglia**

MINESTRONE SOUP

There is really no recipe for minestrone soup. I recall that it all started with some water and a bag of meat bones which Mama usually got free from the butcher. (He later began to charge her a few pennies for them, which she thought was outrageous.) To the bones boiling away in the water she would add vegetables: onions, tomatoes, cabbage, carrots, beans, peas, garlic (of course!) and pastas of various shapes and sizes. I always suspected that, as with all recipes Mama cooked, there was a special secret ingredient. In this case I noticed that when the soup began to lose its flavor, or became too thick, she'd add a generous splash of wine, stir it and leave it to continue its slow, gentle simmer.*

*Reprinted with permission from *Bus 9 to Paradise*, Leo F. Buscaglia, Slack Incorporated, 1986.

JEAN KASEM
Actress

Mother: Irene Thompson

My mother was an Iroquois Indian, and many of her dishes were handed down from our ancestors. We ate my favorite meal every Sunday, when she made light and fluffy Indian doughcakes, served with fresh fruit or preserves.

Doughcakes are what the Indians in New England used to keep the colonists alive when they first arrived on these shores. They're very versatile and can be served hot or cold, even with maple syrup. I took them to school cold in my lunch box.

I make them the modern way, with Pillsbury Hot Roll Mix, because it rises much faster. Just make up the dough, cut it into irregular shapes and put a slit in the middle with a sharp knife. Fry in hot oil and watch them puff up!

But doughcakes weren't my only favorite. Nothing could warm me up faster than my mother's hearty vegetable soup.

—Jean Kasem

VEGETABLE SOUP

3/4 lb. fresh green beans or 1 box frozen green beans

1 green pepper, seeded and chopped

1/2 large or 1 whole small cauliflower, cut into flowerets

6 stalks (ribs) of sliced celery

1/4 cup chopped parsley or celery leaves

2-4 large yellow onions, sliced or chopped

1 16 oz. can peeled tomatoes

1 16 oz. can V-8 juice

4 pkg. MBT chicken broth or 4 large cans chicken broth

2 tsp. thyme

1 pkg. frozen whole baby okra (optional)

Mix all ingredients and simmer for 15 minutes. This recipe makes a large pot of soup that will keep for two weeks in the refrigerator.

Although everyone has the Constitutional right to complain, you will find neither a reason to filibuster nor a kitchen appliance in this chowder, a favorite from Barbara Bush. . . .

BARBARA (MRS. GEORGE) BUSH

Active volunteer and wife of Vice-President George Bush

Mother: Pauline (Robinson) Pierce

ALL-AMERICAN CLAM CHOWDER

3 slices bacon
1/2 cup minced onions
7 1/2 oz. can minced clams (save clam liquor)

1 cup cubed potatoes
1 can cream of celery soup
1 1/2 cups milk
dash of pepper

Cook bacon in frying pan until crisp. Remove, drain and break into one-inch pieces. Brown onion in bacon fat. Add clam liquor and potatoes. Cover and cook over low heat until potatoes are done (about 15 minutes). Blend in bacon pieces, minced clams, and other ingredients. Heat, but do *not* boil. Bacon may be used for garnish. Serves 3.

LEE IACOCCA

Chairman of the Board, Chief Executive Officer, Chrysler Corporation

Mother: Antoinette (Perrotto) Iacocca

Of all the world's great Neapolitan cooks, my mother has to be one of the best.

—Lee Iacocca

ANTOINETTE IACOCCA'S
ITALIAN MEATBALL SOUP

1 stewing chicken or large fryer,
 about 4 lbs.
1 medium onion, quartered
1 large carrot, cut in chunks
1 large rib celery, cut in chunks
cold water
salt and freshly ground pepper
 to taste

1 lb. fine-ground veal
1 large egg
1½ tbl. grated Parmesan
 cheese
1 tbl. minced fresh parsley
½ lb. small pasta squares
additional grated Parmesan
 cheese

In large soup kettle or pot, combine chicken, onion, carrot and celery. Cover with cold water and bring to a boil. Season with salt and pepper to taste and simmer about two hours, until stock is reduced and chicken is very tender. Remove chicken and strain stock into large bowl. Skim off most of fat on top. Remove meat from chicken bones. Shred enough chicken to make one cup; add to stock. (Save remaining chicken for another recipe, such as chicken salad.)

In medium bowl, combine veal, egg, Parmesan cheese and parsley; mix thoroughly and form into tiny meatballs about the size of a large marble.

Return de-fatted stock to pot and bring to a boil. Drop in meatballs and pasta squares and simmer 20 minutes. Ladle into soup bowls and sprinkle with grated Parmesan. Makes about 8-10 servings.

ESTHER BLUMENFELD

Author, lecturer

Mother: Ruth May Richter

When I was a child, every skinned knee and sniffle was soothed with a cup of Mama's chicken soup. And later, in college, dreams of home and soup gave me incentive to study at final exam time.

So when I asked my mom for the recipe, I was shocked at how easy it is to prepare. Incredulous, I asked, "Are you sure this is all there is to it?" Although she had never written it down, she swore by these ingredients.

After the third, "Are you sure you haven't left anything out? This is too easy," Dad finally interrupted. "Daughter, if you want to complicate it, you can always throw in a dead squirrel."

I don't recommend the dead squirrel, but this just might be the best and easiest chicken soup in the world.

—**Esther Blumenfeld**

RUTH RICHTER'S EASY & DELICIOUS
CHICKEN SOUP

1 small chicken, quartered; or
   chicken pieces
16-oz. can of mixed vegetables

6 chicken bouillon cubes
salt to taste

Pour 4 quarts of water into a pot and add remaining ingredients. Let the mixture boil until the chicken is tender; leave the pot covered.

Remove the chicken pieces and strain the soup through a sieve. Let it cool and place it into the refrigerator overnight. In the morning, remove the layer of fat from the surface.

This makes a clear broth. Add noodles, serve and stay healthy! The leftover soup may be frozen for future use.

Mother: Tzveta (Dimitrova) Javacheva

   The following recipe was prepared by my mother, Tzveta Javacheva, born Dimitrova, on warm summer nights in Bulgaria. This refreshing and healthy dish is a great appetizer or can be a meal when served with bread. My wife, Jeanne-Claude, learned this recipe from me and often prepares it as an appetizer for our summer guests.

—Christo

TARATOR (SUMMER SOUP)

4 8 oz. containers of plain
   lowfat yogurt
1 cup of walnuts, each walnut
   cut into 8 pieces
1/2 cup dill

2 tbl. olive oil
2 tbl. vinegar
4 large cucumbers, raw, diced as
   small as possible
1 tsp. salt

Mix all ingredients together and refrigerate for at least 3 hours before serving. Serves 6.

☆ ☆ ☆

My friend, Dian, is an imaginative cook, but it took several years to wean her husband from his meat-and-potatoes upbringing. No matter what she served, either he or their young children would voice objections to the whole dish, the spices, or an offending ingredient. Dian finally got fed up.

"I cook dinner seven days a week without any help, and I don't want to hear any more complaints about *anything*."

The next night, halfway through dinner, Dian bit down on something bland, pale green, and unchewable in her salad. "What in the world is this?" she muttered, holding up the mystery morsel . . . a piece of paper toweling. "I can't believe I tore up the paper towel along with the drained lettuce. Why didn't anyone say anything?"

"Well," confessed her husband sheepishly, "I thought it was an awfully strange new lettuce, but then I remembered how upset you got last night and I decided I was better off eating it!"

— LA

JIMMY CARTER
President of the United States, 1977-81

Mother: Lillian (Gordy) Carter

For fifty years, my mother, "Miss Lillian," was a member of the Plains Stitch 'n Chat Club, which met every other Wednesday at one of the members' homes for an hour of hand sewing and conversation, followed by super refreshments (and more conversation).

Usually a congealed salad, sweet, and sandwich were served. Here's her recipe for a lime congealed salad which was her favorite. She doubled the recipe to serve the fifteen members.

—Jimmy Carter

LIME CONGEALED SALAD

1 3 oz. pkg. lime Jello
1 cup hot water
1 cup small marshmallows
1 cup (drained) crushed
  pineapple

³/₄ cup chopped pecans
1 cup whipping cream
6 oz. cream cheese, softened at
  room temperature

Dissolve Jello in hot water. Refrigerate. When it cools and starts to congeal, add marshmallows, pineapple and pecans. In separate bowl, whip cream 'til it forms soft peaks. Stir into softened cream cheese.

Fold into Jello mixture, spread in 9″ x 9″ square pan. Refrigerate until set. Cut into squares and serve on lettuce leaves. (Can be decorated with a blob of mayonnaise topped with a cherry.) Serves 8.

JANE ALEXANDER
Actress, Tony and Emmy Award winner

Mother: Ruth (Pearson) Quigley

My father was the doctor for the Harvard football team. From the time I was a young girl, massive young men would be seated at our beautiful Sunday lunch table. These football players would eat gargantuan portions of food, which pleased my mother no end: roasts of beef, bowls of my grandmother's cucumber salad, dozens of rolls.

As time went by, my mother came to believe that *everyone* should consume the same amount as these athletes, and felt wounded if a guest or one of us did not have second or even *third* helpings of food. It's a wonder that I didn't grow up to be a giant myself!

—Jane Alexander

CUCUMBER & ONION SALAD

3 cucumbers
1 small onion
1 tsp. sugar

$^1/_2$ cup sour cream
$^1/_2$ cup vinegar

Peel and slice cucumbers very thin. Slice the onion very thin. Layer cukes and onion slices in bowl, salting liberally. Press mixture to remove liquid by using a plate with a pitcher of water on it or some other similar device to weight down the plate. Leave them pressed 3-4 hours, draining liquid occasionally.

Prepare a sauce of sugar, sour cream and vinegar, varying proportions to taste. Should be a sweet/sour taste. Mix well with drained cukes and onions.

RICHARD G. LUGAR

U.S. Senator from Indiana

Mother: Bertha (Green) Lugar

I recall, from my childhood, working around the house with the rest of my family on Saturday afternoons. After our work was finished, we gathered around the table to enjoy the wonderful meals my mother prepared. I always looked forward to a hearty Hoosier dinner.

—**Richard Lugar**

LUGAR'S PASTA SALAD

1 lb. spaghetti
1 green pepper
1 bunch green onions
2 ribs celery

2 tomatoes
1 cucumber
1 8-oz. bottle Italian dressing
1 jar McCormick's "Salad Supreme"

Break spaghetti into bite-sized pieces and cook just until tender. Drain pasta. Chop vegetables finely. Add all other ingredients and mix together while pasta is still warm.

This pasta salad is best when made a day ahead and refrigerated. Serve cold or at room temperature. Will feed 15-20 people as a side dish. Ideal dish for a potluck supper.

PAUL ANKA

Singer, composer, winner of 15 gold records

Mother: Camilia (Tannis) Anka

As a youngster, when I arrived home from school, my mother would *always* be cooking. I especially remember when she was preparing my favorite, Taboulay, a wheat germ (Bourghol) and parsley salad. Naturally, I would fetch my stool and bother her until she would let me help (always conditional that my hands had been washed clean). She would allow me to chop the parsley, cube the tomatoes, and dice the scallions (according to her strict specifications).

All in all, I still remember quite a bit of her teachings and I still prepare these dishes when I am at home. Equal in my memory, I remember that my dad was in the restaurant business and I used to go to the restaurant and poke around the kitchen, bothering the chefs to explain certain dishes and recipes.

I consider myself a good cook and enjoy preparing meals. I find it relaxes me and gives me a much needed respite from an intense performance schedule.

—**Paul Anka**

TABOULAY (PARSLEY SALAD)

2 bunches parsley
2 medium, ripe tomatoes
1/2 cup cracked wheat (Bourghol,
  also known as bulgur)
4 scallions

2 tbl. pure olive oil
juice of one fresh lemon
salt and pepper to taste
leaves of 2 heads romaine
lettuce

Thoroughly wash parsley. Separate and throw away stems. Chop parsley fine (knife-chop only). Cube tomatoes. Soak Bourghol for 2 hours in water, then squeeze water out of Bourghol. Dice scallions, including 1″ of the green tops.

Place all these ingredients in a salad bowl. Then add olive oil, lemon juice, salt and pepper. Mix it well with two spoons. Place in refrigerator overnight or for seven hours before serving. Wash lettuce leaves and place leaves on a platter. To serve, place salad on leaves. Enjoy! Serves 4.

ANA-ALICIA

Actress

Mother: Alicia Ortiz

My mother was always known for her terrific meatloaf, especially the leftover ones that got chilled and made great sandwiches. One night my older brother came home late, sneaked into the refrigerator and made himself a sandwich.

The next morning Mom asked where the dogfood she'd stored in the refrigerator had gone. He said, "Mom, you know, it wasn't that bad. Amazing what a little lettuce, tomato and mayonnaise can do!"

—Ana-Alicia

CHINESE CHICKEN SALAD

½ lb. boiled chicken
2 oz. rice sticks
oil
4 finely sliced green onions

2 tbl. sliced almonds
2 tbl. toasted sesame seeds
1 head of lettuce, shredded

Ahead of time: Soak cooked chicken in soy sauce for a few hours. When ready to prepare salad, fry rice sticks in hot oil for a few seconds (or use already fried, canned rice noodles, available from La Choy).

Dressing:

¼ cup salad oil
1 tbl. sesame oil (this adds a lot of flavor)
3 tbl. vinegar

1 tsp. salt
¼ tsp. pepper
2 tsp. sugar

Shake well until all ingredients are well mixed, and then toss with salad ingredients. Serves 4.

III

HEADLINERS

(Main Dishes)

Several years ago John Friese, then Director of Food Services at Kent State University, was invited by the Virginia Military Institute to advise them on the quality of their meals.

Trying to appear as inconspicuous as possible, he leaned against the cafeteria wall, watching as the students picked up each food-laden tray which rolled briskly down a long conveyor belt. Marveling at the inventiveness of the hidden chef, he realized that he had never seen so much reconstructed, re-shaped and compressed food. He could only guess what most of the items must have been in their natural state before undergoing culinary metamorphosis.

Upon closer examination, he spied a grayish slice of liver curling over the edge of one of the orbiting trays. Whipping his food thermometer out of his pocket, he stuck it into the center of the meat — standard testing procedure. At that moment, however, someone distracted him and the tray got away before he could remove it from the revolving belt.

As the meat sailed by with the thermometer still in place, a student picked up the tray and quizzically studied his lunch. "Well," he concluded, "I always knew the meat was sick, but I never knew it ran a fever."

—EB

MONTY HALL

Television producer, actor

Mother: Rose (Rusen) Halparin

My mother combined her great insight into human nature with her cooking talent. When we were first married, my bride, Marilyn, faced a tremendous challenge in equaling my mother's reputation as an outstanding cook — without success. I urged Marilyn to get my mother's recipes, and then we invited Mother over to cook her specialty for us. The dish was a fiasco. I was nonplussed. How had it tasted so good when I was a boy? What had happened?

But my mother's brilliant mind had conceived a plan to make my wife's cooking look good by comparison. She had deliberately cooked everything just a little off. She threw the game!

Later she revealed the missing ingredient to Marilyn so that it would taste better the next time, and Marilyn would get all the credit!

—Monty Hall

43

SWEET AND SOUR STEWED TONGUE

1 fresh beef tongue
water to cover
1 tbl. salt
1 onion, sliced
6 whole cloves
6 peppercorns
2 bay leaves
1 onion, chopped fine
1 tbl. fat

1 tbl. flour
2 cups tongue liquid
1 tbl. finely ground almonds
1 stick cinnamon
3 cloves
2 tbl. raisins
1/4 cup brown sugar
1 tbl. molasses
juice of 1 lemon

Place tongue in pot with hot or cold water to cover. Add salt, sliced onion, cloves, peppercorns, bay leaves. Cover pot and let simmer 3-4 hours until tender. (Add hot water if necessary to keep tongue covered during cooking.) Remove from heat; let tongue stand in liquid until cool enough to handle. Peel off outer skin, trim off root and return tongue to liquid. When ready to serve, set aside 2 cups tongue liquid and slice the tongue.

Sauté chopped onion in fat until onion is golden. Sprinkle flour over onion. Cook, stirring for a few minutes. Gradually add 2 cups tongue liquid, stirring constantly. Cook and stir 5 minutes 'til mixture is well blended and slightly thickened. Add almonds, cinnamon, 3 cloves and raisins. Combine well. Add brown sugar, molasses and lemon juice. Cook and stir 10 minutes longer.

Correct seasoning, adding more salt, sugar and lemon juice if desired. Add sliced tongue. Heat thoroughly and serve immediately in the sauce. Serves 4.*

*Recipe reprinted, with permission, from *The Celebrity Kosher Cookbook*, by Marilyn Hall and Rabbi Jerome Cutler, J. P. Tarcher, Inc.

DEE WALLACE STONE

Actress

Mother: Maxine Bowers

The following is the recipe for my mother's famous Beef Brisket. We had it at all our special holiday celebrations, except the Easter when our German shepherd, Hobo, climbed to the table where it was waiting and proceeded to devour the *entire* brisket! We sent out for chicken that Easter.

And ever after, whenever we serve brisket, we always make a toast to Hobo — and Mother's patience!

—Dee Wallace Stone

BRISKET

1 beef brisket
celery salt
garlic salt
onion salt

barbecue salt
salt and pepper
$^1/_2$ to 1 bottle Liquid Smoke

SAUCE

1 bottle chili sauce
1 cup ketchup

$1^1/_2$ cups barbecue sauce

Preheat oven to 250-300. Trim off excess fat. Line a long pan with foil. Pound and jab brisket to tenderize. Place in pan, fat side up. Sprinkle with seasoned salts. Add a little salt and pepper. Pour Liquid Smoke over meat. Add a little water to cover bottom of pan. Wrap in foil tightly and place in oven. If it is a large brisket, you can cook it overnight, or 4-5 hours.

Then pour off most of the liquid, cool and make sauce: Mix chili sauce, ketchup and barbecue sauce well and pour over meat. Cover and return to oven for 1-2 hours. This is also great for barbecue ribs. Cook 3 hours, same as above, in 300-350 oven. Enjoy!

LEWIS GRIZZARD

Newspaper columnist, author, humorist

Mother: Christine Atkinson

The French fry is a marvelous creation. I think that perhaps God Himself created the French fry, say on about the twelfth or thirteenth day. And it was good. French fries stayed that way for several thousand years, but then modern man started monkeying with them.

I suspect God is quite angry about it, and that may be one reason why the weather has been so loused up lately.

My mother, a devout Methodist, could prepare wonderful French fries. She would take out potatoes and cut them just like I liked them — long and thin — and she would fry them in a pan, the grease popping out on her arms and hands the entire time. She also would fry them just like I liked them — crispy on the outside, soggy and greasy on the inside.

I find myself craving the food my mother reared me on. I still eat lunch at my mother's house once a week. She always apologizes when I walk in.

"Son, we don't have hardly anything to eat today," she says.

So what am I going to get here? A piece of toast and a radish? Then I go to the table and there's enough food to feed the Chinese infantry: country fried steak smothered in gravy, mashed potatoes with no lumps in them, all sorts of fresh vegetables from the garden, hot cornbread and maybe even some coconut pie.*

COUNTRY FRIED STEAK

1 lb. round steak, 1/2" thick
1/2 cup flour

salt and pepper
2 cups water, more if necessary

Pound steak with the edge of a plate to tenderize. Add salt and pepper to flour, then dredge steak in the mixture. Using a heavy skillet, barely cover the bottom with grease. Over high heat, brown both sides of the steak. When brown, turn heat to low.

Pour in enough water to cover steak, cover with a lid and cook slowly for one hour. Check every 15 minutes and add more water if necessary. The pan liquids will make your gravy. Serves 3-4.

*Reprinted from *Elvis Is Dead, and I Don't Feel So Good Myself*, by permission of Peachtree Publishers, Ltd.

EDWARD I. KOCH

Mayor of New York City

Mother: Joyce Silpe

My mother's hamburgers were my favorite meal. Since we were poor, her recipe was unique. The ingredients were as follows: 70 percent chopped beef, 10 percent onion, 5 percent garlic and 15 percent crackermeal. The secret was to deep fry the burgers in chicken fat. Today such a meal would kill you, but in my youth I couldn't wait to wolf them down!

—Ed Koch

MARY KAY ASH

Founder, Mary Kay Cosmetics

Mother: Lula (Vember) Wagner

My mother was a wonderful cook, and I think she is most remembered for her fantastic chicken and dumplings. We all looked forward to Sunday dinner, week after week, year after year.

I was born in Hot Wells, Texas, where my mother and father owned a hotel. Every Sunday it became the "thing to do" to go to Hot Wells for Sunday dinner and have my mother's fabulous chicken and dumplings; and, of course, to take baths in the warm springs there. When my father became ill, she had to give up the hotel in Hot Wells. We then moved to Houston, where she became a chef in a restaurant, making chicken and dumplings the most favorite meal on the menu.

—Mary Kay Ash

CHICKEN AND DUMPLINGS

1 stewing chicken
1 cup milk
2 eggs

salt
2½-3 cups flour, or more

Cut up one stewing chicken and boil until tender, approximately 2 hours. Salt broth to taste.

For dumplings: Combine milk, eggs and salt. Stir in 2½-3 cups flour, or enough that you can knead the dough without it sticking to your hands. Roll dough paper thin and cut into 1″ strips. Boil 15 minutes in chicken broth. Serve immediately. Serves 4.

Baked, fried or smothered in sauce, chicken has become the "grin-'n-bear-it" staple for both politicians and ministers. As for my father, a rabbi, the Good Lord tested him with this ubiquitous fowl yet again when, after conducting a funeral, Dad went to the house of mourning for his usual condolence call.

The sister of the deceased elderly lady insisted that he have a bite to eat. "Rabbi," she urged, "you must eat a piece of this chicken."

Just as he sank his teeth into a juicy drumstick, she added, "Our dear, departed Minnie baked it with her own hands, right before she passed on. Eat hearty!"

—EB

DR. NORMAN VINCENT PEALE

Clergyman, author

Mother: Anna (DeLaney) Peale

Through the years, another clergyman, Dr. Norman Vincent Peale, has done a lot of hearty chicken eating himself. For him, no lingering taste of the most elaborate chicken compares to the memories stirred up by his mother's simple Chicken Fricassee. . . .

I fondly remember the fricassee chicken my mother prepared and served often.
—Dr. Norman Vincent Peale

CHICKEN FRICASSEE

4-5 lb. chicken
flour
shortening

3 cups water
salt
2 ribs celery

Rinse chicken, cut into serving pieces, and pat dry. Coat chicken with flour and brown in fat. Add 3 cups water, salt and cut-up celery. Cover and simmer until fork tender. Strain and reserve broth to make gravy.

MILK GRAVY

2 tbl. butter
6 tbl. flour
3/4 cup milk

1 1/4 cups chicken broth
salt and pepper to taste
4 tbl. light cream

Melt butter in saucepan. Add flour and cook over low heat, stirring constantly. Stir in chicken broth and milk, cooking 8-10 minutes until sauce thickens. Add salt and pepper to taste and stir in cream. This fricassee was always served with mashed potatoes. Serves 6.

CAPTAIN GENE CERNAN

Apollo 17 astronaut, last man to leave footprints on the moon

Mother: Rose A. Cernan

There is no truth to the rumor that NASA compressed the following recipe into a tube for our moon walkers, but astronaut Cernan thought it was well worth the trip back to earth. . . .

CHICKEN SPAGHETTI

1/2 cup olive oil
4 small cans tomato paste
2 cloves garlic
1 tbl. chopped parsley
1/2 tsp. black pepper
1 tbl. sugar

1 medium onion, chopped
1 tbl. sweet basil
2 tbl. salt
1 large fryer or chicken breasts
4 cans water (tomato paste cans)

Cut fryer in pieces. Sauté chopped onion, garlic, spices and chicken in large pot containing olive oil, stirring well to coat chicken. Then cover and cook slowly, about 20 minutes.

Add tomato paste and water, stir well. Cook over medium heat, partially covered, until sauce is thick and chicken is tender — about 45 minutes. If sauce needs to thicken more, lift chicken out with slotted spoon and cook sauce about 15 minutes longer. Serve over cooked spaghetti. Serves 4-6.

GERALDINE A. FERRARO

Attorney, former N.Y. Congresswoman, first woman V-P nominee

Mother: Antonetta (Corrieri) Ferraro

Though this manicotti is not my mom's recipe, it is one of her favorite dishes. In fact, I have few of her recipes I can even pass on to my children. Learning to cook from my mother was not an experience which lent itself to continuity between generations. I would stand by the table as she mixed ingredients for a favorite dish, with proportions measured out as "a handful of this, and a pinch of that, and just a little — this much — of the other." Of course, when I was ten and my hands were as little as hers, it was fine.

As I grew, unfortunately, so did my hands. My children, especially my son who is the gourmet cook in our family, all are bigger than I.

I've made this recipe so long that my mom is convinced I got it from her!

I have two comments about this recipe: (1) You'll need tomato sauce as you get to the final step of preparation for baking. I make a "from scratch" Bolognese meat sauce (but my family is spoiled) and I make a lot. So what I don't use on the manicotti, I save. You can use any of the prepared spaghetti sauces — start out with one jar, if you need another, use the second; (2) This recipe is time-consuming but well worth it. If followed carefully, you will have the best manicotti this side of the Atlantic!

—Geraldine Ferraro

MANICOTTI PANCAKES

1 cup all purpose flour	¼ tsp. salt
1 cup water	4 eggs

Combine flour, water and salt and beat until smooth. Beat in eggs *one at a time*. Heat a 5-6″ skillet and grease with a few drops of oil. Put about 3 tablespoons batter in hot skillet and roll pan around to distribute evenly. Cook over low heat until firm. *Do not brown*. Turn and cook lightly on other side. Continue making pancakes until all batter is used. (Do not grease skillet a second time.) Makes 12-14 pancakes.

MANICOTTI FILLING

½ tsp. salt
3 eggs
2 lbs. ricotta cheese

¼ cup grated Italian cheese
pepper to taste
1 lb. mozzarella cheese, cut in
strips

Preheat oven to 350. Mix the first five ingredients together for filling. Put about two tablespoons filling and a strip of mozzarella on each pancake and roll up. Pour your tomato sauce on the bottom of a large shallow baking dish, just to cover. Put pancakes seam side down in dish. Cover with more sauce and sprinkle with grated cheese. Bake in 350 oven for 45 minutes.

The pancakes may be made the day before and refrigerated. On the day you serve, just fill and bake. If you make pancakes the day before, put wax paper between them to prevent sticking.

When serving, you should have additional sauce and grated cheese available to add, according to individual taste. Serves 4-6.

PAT BOONE

Singer, actor

Mother: Margaret (Prichard) Boone

Pat and Shirley Boone's Chili-Mac, having long ago survived its trial by fire, has been seasoned by their marriage of over 35 years. . . .

CHILI-MAC FROM THE BOONE KITCHEN

1 lb. ground beef
2 medium onions, chopped
2 15-oz. cans tomato sauce
chili powder
salt

2 15-oz. cans solid packed tomatoes
2 15-oz. cans red kidney beans
2 oz. per person, uncooked
spaghetti
2 tbl. Wesson oil

Cook onions in Wesson oil until tender. Add ground beef to skillet and cook until brown. Add beef and onions to tomatoes, beans and sauce in a large container. Cook spaghetti and add it, then season to taste with salt and chili powder. Simmer for one hour.

CHEESE SAUCE

1 cup sharp Cheddar cheese
1 cup sour cream

garlic salt
spring onions, chopped

Grate cheese. Combine ingredients in saucepan and warm slowly over low heat, just enough to melt cheese. Sprinkle a little garlic salt in this sauce to your taste. Serve on the side of chili-mac with chopped spring onions as well. Serves 6-8.

IRVING WALLACE
Author

Mother: Bessie (Liss) Wallace

The origins of "Hamburger Pudding à la I.W.," as I like to call it, are lost in French history. The basic recipe, since refined, was brought to us by a clever and inventive French housekeeper-cook who came to our employ from a suburb of Paris twenty-five years ago. With this secret recipe from our family, we promise you ecstatic cluckings over a dish to love.

—Irving Wallace

HAMBURGER PUDDING À LA I.W.

1 small onion
4 large potatoes
³/₄ lb. ground meat

All-Seasoning
salt and pepper
milk

Boil potatoes until soft. Meanwhile, chop the onion, but not too finely. Brown in butter. Add the ground beef. Into the mixture, add a dash of salt, a dash of pepper, a dash of All-Seasoning. Leave uncovered and cook slowly for 20 minutes. As you cook, continue to break up the ground meat.

Now, having cooked the potatoes, mash them tenderly, evenly, adding a modest portion of milk. Take out a glass casserole. Fill the bottom with a thin layer of mashed potatoes. On top of this, spread all of the meat mixture. Then, atop this, spread with remaining mashed potatoes.

Place the casserole in a broiler and brown the pudding slowly. About 40 minutes, low flame, will produce a deep crust. Present the dish steaming hot, serving the pudding in slices or scoops. Serves 4-6. Voilà!

BOB GRIESE

Sportscaster, former professional football player, Miami Dolphins

Mother: Ida Griese

Bob had a weird habit — he liked to dunk peanut butter sandwiches in his chili. One day Bob and his older brother, Bill, were playing basketball in the kitchen with a dirty old tennis ball. The basket was a cut-out shoe box tacked over the door.

One time the ball missed the shoe box, hit the door frame instead and ricocheted right into the chili pot as I was stirring it, splashing chili all over the stove, the floor and me. Needless to say, I was furious.

That night we had peanut butter sandwiches *without* the chili. No way could I have served my family that chili after his "basketball" landed in it. That was the dirtiest, nastiest tennis ball I had ever seen!

—Ida Griese

IDA GRIESE'S CHILI

1½ lbs. ground beef
1 medium onion, chopped
1 green pepper, chopped
2 cans Joan of Arc red kidney
beans

2 cans water
1 medium can tomato paste
chili powder
salt and pepper to taste

In skillet combine onion, green pepper and ground beef. Cook until meat is done. In large kettle combine beans, water and tomato paste.

Drain ground beef mixture and add to beans. Stir in chili powder, salt and pepper to taste. Cover and cook over medium heat for about 1½ hours, stirring often. When the beans soften, I take my potato masher and "mash" the chili. The pulp from the beans helps thicken the chili. If necessary, add water. Serves 4-6.

JOE MONTANA

Professional football player, San Francisco 49'ers

Mother: Theresa Montana

This recipe will feed ten kindergartners, eight regular adults, or one unforgettable quarterback. . . .

MONTANA RAVIOLI

Meat filling:

2 lbs. hamburger meat
1 pkg. frozen chopped spinach
1 medium onion, chopped
2 eggs, beaten

¼ to ½ cup Romano cheese, grated
salt and pepper to taste

Thaw and drain spinach. Brown meat and onion in skillet with a little butter. Add spinach and mix. Remove from heat and add eggs and Romano cheese.

Dough:

7 cups flour	3 eggs
1 tbl. salt	1 cup water

Mix ingredients together. Dough should be soft and smooth, not sticky.

Divide dough in half. Roll one half of dough as for a large pie crust. Place a tablespoon of filling once every 2″ on the rolled out dough, making sure to make uniform rows of filling. Roll second half of dough as for a large pie crust. Carefully place dough over rows of filling.

Cut ravioli into squares. Pinch edges of each square. Drop into boiling water and cook 6-8 minutes. Remove from water and place on serving dish. Top with spaghetti sauce. Serves 6-8.

One of my favorite recipes, albeit different, is one which I originally received from Senator Ted Stevens called "Ann Stevens' Dishwasher Fish." The recipe is simple!

—Howard Baker, White House Chief of Staff

TED STEVENS
U.S. Senator from Alaska

Mother: Gertrude (Chancellor) Stevens

In Alaska, the fish are so plentiful and obliging that if you live near a stream, all you have to do is open a window and whistle and they'll leap into the nearest appliance. Senator Stevens' late wife, Ann, known for her charm and wit, always surprised her guests when she pulled this family specialty from her dishwasher.

ANN STEVENS'S DISHWASHER FISH

fish fillets   butter
salt   fresh lemon juice

Place fish fillets on aluminum foil that has been doubled over. Season with salt, butter and lemon juice to taste. Wrap the fish fillets tightly in foil and place in the dishwasher. Turn the dishwasher on and let it run through the entire cycle. The heat and steam from the hot water provide for a tasty dinner. The fish tastes better if the detergent is left out of the recipe!

It is character building for a child to help out around the house. And it was especially vital in Robin's family, where her mother Rita was working outside the home writing a food column called "Twirl the Lazy Susan." Thus eight-year-old Robin had a few small chores to do after school.

One afternoon as she was setting the dinner table, Rita phoned to explain that she was delayed. "Robin, please wash the carrots and lettuce." Twenty minutes later Rita's phone rang with an exasperated daughter on the line. "Mother," she wailed, "I dunked and I dunked, but the soap won't come out. How do I get the lettuce to stop bubbling?"

—**EB**

CLINT EASTWOOD

Actor, director, producer, Mayor of Carmel, California

Mother: Ruth Eastwood

When Dirty Harry Callahan says, "Come clean," he's not talking lettuce. However, a light soapless salad would be the perfect accompaniment to Clint Eastwood's prize-winning Spaghetti Western. . . .

SPAGHETTI WESTERN

juice of 1 lemon
12 tbl. olive oil
12 baby artichokes
 2 large cloves garlic, diced
¼ cup finely chopped celery
¼ cup chopped shallots
½ cup tomato puree
½ cup fish stock
salt and freshly ground pepper
¼ tsp. thyme
 1 bay leaf
 2 tbl. chopped parsley
saffron

 2 tbl. tomato paste
½ tsp. anchovy paste
 4 clams, chopped
 4 Monterey Bay prawns or
jumbo shrimp
12 large mussels
½ cup brandy
 1 yellow pepper, thinly sliced
 1 red pepper, thinly sliced
2½ tbl. Pernod
½ cup heavy cream
½ lb. spaghetti, raw
 8 large sea scallops, quartered

Stir juice from ½ lemon and 2 tablespoons olive oil into a large pot of salted boiling water. Add artichokes and boil for 5 minutes, or until almost tender. Remove artichokes and cool under cold running water. Reserve artichoke cooking water. Peel outer leaves from 8 artichokes down to tenderest part (leave 4 artichokes with leaves intact). Cut off stem. Cut peeled artichokes into bite-size pieces (about 1½″ long). Set aside.

Add additional salted water to leftover artichoke water, bring to a boil and cook pasta. Drain and return to pot.

In a large skillet heat 7 tablespoons olive oil; sauté garlic, celery, two tablespoons shallots until golden brown. Add tomato purée, fish stock, salt and pepper, thyme, bay leaf, parsley, two generous pinches saffron, tomato paste, anchovy paste and clams. Bring to a low simmer and cover.

In a large skillet heat 3 tablespoons olive oil and sauté two tablespoons chopped shallots. Season with black pepper. Add prawns and mussels, cover with brandy and ignite. Remove from heat and when flame subsides, set aside.

Add red and yellow peppers, artichokes, mussels and brandy to sauce and simmer 5 minutes. Add Pernod and cream to sauce and cook one minute, stirring constantly. Remove from heat.

Using a slotted spoon, remove peppers from sauce, add to spaghetti. Rinse the spaghetti/pepper mixture in hot water and drain (this is to remove traces of the sauce).

Cover the bottom of 4 flat bowls with a few tablespoons sauce. Divide the spaghetti among the bowls, leaving a hollow in the center. Place 2 quartered raw scallops in the center. Arrange 3 mussels on edge of each plate and, on the opposite side, place 3 artichokes. On each plate, place a reserved, uncut artichoke over the scallops. Spoon remaining sauce over scallops and mussels. Place one prawn in center. If preparing in advance, cover with foil and set aside. To serve, reheat in 325 oven for 20 minutes. Serves 4.

JAKE STEINFELD

Bodybuilder to the stars, "Body by Jake," television performer

Mother: Joy Steinfeld

My mom is a mom's mom — caring, loving, a real friend to everyone. She works at Universal Studios, so everybody there knows her. Everything she does, including cooking, she does in a big way — she's very cool.

Last year she gave me a surprise twenty-ninth birthday party and invited all my friends, including Steven Spielberg, Harrison Ford, Terri Garr and Priscilla Presley. They all like her — she is a real old-fashioned mom, straight and very funny. I thought the surprise party was for Dad, so I spent the day keeping him out of the house. Turned out I was keeping myself out of the house!

One thing about our family dinners when I was growing up, we always had salad, grapefruit or melon, meat, vegetable, potatoes and dessert. Every night was an affair, a mini-Bar Mitzvah.

When I was in junior high school I liked to scare my mom. She made my lunch each night after watching Johnny Carson, and I'd sneak up behind her when the refrigerator door was open. I'd wait behind the door, sometimes for as long as ten minutes while she worked, until she shut the door. "Excuse me!" I'd shout. It scared her every time. "One day you'll give me a heart attack," she'd scold, "and then you won't have lunch."

My all-time favorite dish is her Shrimp Parmigiana, served with spaghetti or ziti. Now, whenever I want to impress a girl, I invite her to my parents' home for dinner. I call Mom and say, "I'm bringing a date to dinner. S.P., Mom!"

—Jake Steinfeld

SHRIMP PARMIGIANA

1 lb. fresh shrimp, peeled
seasoned bread crumbs
2 eggs, beaten

2 tbl. butter or margarine
2 tbl. olive oil

Boil peeled shrimp 2-3 minutes, depending on size. Drain and pat dry. Coat shrimp first in eggs, then in bread crumbs. Brown breaded shrimp in butter and oil.

SAUCE

1½ lb. ground sirloin
1 15-oz. can tomato sauce
1 6-oz. can tomato paste

1 cup water
½ cup grated Parmesan cheese

Preheat oven to 350. Brown meat. Pour off fat. Add tomato sauce, tomato paste and water. Stir until thoroughly blended. Arrange shrimp in casserole dish. Cover with sauce. Sprinkle with Parmesan cheese. Bake in 350 for 20-25 minutes. Serves 6.

MARY HEALY

Singer, actress

Mother: Viola (Armbruster) Healy

I remember Mama doing her housework and then rushing off to work in an office. You see, my dad died at the age of twenty-seven, leaving my dear mom with four little children. I was the baby and just six months old. You can bet we all had our duties to perform at an early age.

I also remember going to a cooking school when I was about nine and loving it. My first effort of any success was a baked apple stuffed with raisins, which I couldn't resist sampling. And after walking several blocks with this culinary success, I had about two raisins left when my mom received it! Cooking always pleased me, because I found it creative and rewarding.

As the years went by my husband, Peter Lind Hayes, and I enjoyed a very busy career in show business, TV, movies and radio. And with two children, my time was not often spent in the kitchen. However, one meal I always enjoy sharing with friends even today is one Mom used to make. It is especially good for casual dining and can be prepared ahead of time and simply heated whenever you are ready. I usually serve it with rice (I prefer brown) and a big salad.

—Mary Healy

SHRIMP CREOLE

2 lbs. fresh shrimp, cleaned and cooked
1 onion, peeled and sliced
1 green pepper, cut fine
1/2 cup sliced celery
1/2 bay leaf
2 tbl. butter or margarine

3 cups cooked rice, hot
1 tbl. flour
3 cups fresh or canned tomatoes, chopped
1 tsp. salt
1/4 tsp. sugar
touch of cayenne pepper

Sauté onion, green pepper, celery and bay leaf in butter or margarine for 8 minutes. Add flour and stir, mixing smoothly for 2-3 minutes. Add tomatoes, salt, sugar and cayenne pepper (optional).

Mix and let simmer 15 minutes. Add cooked shrimp. Let simmer only until shrimp are hot. *Do not boil* because shrimp will get tough. Serve over bed of hot rice. Excellent for buffet or main dinner dish. Serve in covered casserole. Makes 4-6 servings.

DEBBIE REYNOLDS

Actress, performer

Mother: Maxene Reynolds

Whether showing us *How The West Was Won*, having a *Catered Affair* or leaving a fellow *Singing In The Rain*, El Paso's favorite daughter always lights up when hearing those *Three Little Words* . . . Mama's Taco Pie.

TACO PIE

1/2 lb. lean ground beef
1 12 oz. can Mexican style chili beans
1 4 oz. can chopped green chilies
1 cup shredded longhorn cheese
1 can refrigerated crescent dinner rolls
2 cups shredded lettuce
1 cup chopped tomatoes
sour cream

Preheat oven to 375. Brown ground beef and drain. Add beans and chilies. Simmer about 15 minutes, then add 1/2 cup cheese. Stir until cheese is melted.

Separate crescent rolls and arrange in 9″ glass pie plate so that wide ends form the edge of the pie. Press together. Bake 10 minutes in 375 oven. Spoon meat mixture into crust. Top with lettuce, tomatoes, and rest of cheese.

To serve, cut into wedges and top with a spoonful of sour cream, and guacamole if you like it. Serves 6. Enjoy!

Going out for our weekly family dinner, we arrived at a French restaurant just as it opened. We were the only customers and, as we sat at the table, no one had yet filled our water glasses or told us his name.

Bob finished his pipeful of tobacco and stuck it in his inside coat pocket when our waiter, Bill, arrived to recite the menu and entertain us with a magic trick. He then disappeared into the kitchen.

Five minutes later, as more patrons arrived, the children and I told Bob we smelled smoke. "Maybe they burned something in the kitchen," he said confidently, "but I don't smell anything." "Then why," shouted my son, "is there smoke coming out of your jacket?"

As we all looked on in amazement, Bob nonchalantly pulled open his coat to reveal a smoldering pocket of not-dead-enough pipe embers. Without removing his jacket (there was, after all, a dress code) he stood up and accosted the lethargic waiter who had just exited the kitchen with a pitcher of water. Bob exposed the smoking pocket and calmly asked, "Would you mind pouring that right in here?" After the dumbfounded waiter gave him his fill, Bob then sat down — dripping occasionally — as though nothing had happened.

The four of us had a delicious meal, but the waiter never did forgive Bob for coming up with a magic trick that was better than his.

—**LA**

RICHARD GEPHARDT

U.S. Representative from Missouri

Mother: Loreen Estelle (Cassell) Gephardt

For the ways and means to a flambé-free dinner, fire up this sole recipe from Richard Gephardt. . . .

FILLET OF SOLE

3 lbs. sole (or flounder)
³/₄ cup white wine
1¹/₂ cups water
4 tbl. butter
4 tbl. flour
³/₄ lb. shrimp
chopped green onions

³/₄ cup milk
2 egg yolks
¹/₄ cup cream
lemon juice
salt and pepper
3 tbl. grated Swiss cheese

Preheat oven to 350. Butter bottom of shallow baking dish. Sprinkle with chopped green onions. Lay fillets over them. Season with salt and pepper.

Pour in wine and water to almost cover top of fish. Bring to slow simmer on stove. Cover dish and bake in oven for 10 minutes. Drain off liquid and save for sauce.

Raise oven temperature to 425. In 2-qt. pan melt butter. Add flour. Stir over flame for two minutes. Remove from heat and add poaching liquid and milk. Return to high heat and stir until it thickens and comes to a boil. Let simmer a minute. Mix egg yolks with cream. Stir in two tablespoons of hot mixture and then two more. Add egg and cream mixture to hot sauce and bring to boil over moderate heat. Boil for 30 seconds. Remove from heat.

Add one or two drops lemon juice, salt and pepper. Sauce should lightly coat spoon. If more liquid has accumulated in baking dish, add to sauce. Cover sole with shrimp and then sauce and grated cheese. Bake in top ¹/₃ of oven for 10-15 minutes or until sauce bubbles. Serves 6-8.

VINCE DOOLEY

Athletic director and head football coach, University of Georgia

Mother: Nellie Agnes (Stauter) Dooley

There are several meals that come to mind that Mama prepared when we were young. I recall them so vividly because, now as I look back, they were not only delicious but unique!

Since we were Catholic and lived in a seacoast town, Mobile, we always had seafood on Fridays. We had all types of seafood, but the most memorable was the Crab Omelet Sandwich meals that we had for supper. We also had oyster and shrimp loaves which were delicious. I've tried to get my wife to prepare these delicacies on many occasions, and she has made valiant attempts — but with little success.

We also grew up on raw oysters. We lived only four blocks from the river and every Thursday night my Uncle Wilmer would go down to where the boats came in and get a croker sack full of oysters. He would open them in the back yard in preparation for the Friday meal. About every sixth one that he opened, he would allow us to sample, in secrecy, since it was very much against my mother's wishes. The sampling procedure was simple — he would put the oyster shell to our mouth and we would suck them in the palate.

Sunday dinner (the noon hour) was always the big meal, and many times we had steak and rice and gravy. The meat consisted of round steak (the only steak we ever had) which took approximately two days to tenderize, but when the meal was ready we loved it.

The other unique meal was noodles and prunes. We always had that meal at least once a week, which kept the entire family on a "regular routine."

—**Vince Dooley**

CRAB OMELET SANDWICH

Crabmeat filling:

2 tbl. butter	1 tbl. pimento, diced
1 lb. fresh crabmeat	1 small garlic clove, minced
1 shallot, chopped	dash of Tabasco sauce
1/2 green pepper	salt and pepper to taste

Seed and dice green pepper. Sauté all ingredients in butter for 5 minutes. Cover and set aside.

Omelet:

5 eggs	pinch of pepper
2 tbl. water	2 tbl. butter
$1/2$ tsp. salt	1 small loaf French bread, halved

Slice loaf of French bread lengthwise, spread with butter and warm in low oven. Meanwhile beat remaining ingredients until well blended. Heat skillet until one or two drops of water flicked from fingers sizzle on it. Add butter and tip pan to cover sides and bottom. When thoroughly coated with butter, add omelet mixture, tipping pan back and forth to be sure eggs are evenly distributed. As it cooks, lift edges of omelet with spatula while tipping pan, so uncooked egg will run to the bottom. Cook until mixture is firmly set and bottom is slightly browned.

Spread crabmeat mixture over half of omelet and fold. Remove bread from oven and slide omelet onto bottom half of bread. Cover with top and slice in half. Serves 2.

It doesn't matter whether you're coaching "them Dawgs" or riding herd over Californians, Mama is still bound to ask, "Son, are you eating right?" Not to worry. Obviously, crab lovers Vince Dooley and Governor Deukmejian are doing just fine. . . .

GEORGE DEUKMEJIAN

Governor of California

Mother: Alice (Gairdan) Deukmejian

Both my wife, Gloria, and I hope you enjoy our recipe for Crab Fiesta Bake and will be proud to serve it. It is among the Deukmejian family favorites.

—George Deukmejian

CRAB FIESTA BAKE

1 lb. crabmeat, fresh or frozen
3 cups cooked rice
1/4 lb. Monterey Jack cheese,
   cubed
4 green onions, sliced
2 medium tomatoes, diced

3 tbl. chopped green chilies
1/2 tsp. salt
1/2 tsp. chili powder
1/8 tsp. garlic powder
3/4 cup crushed corn chips

Preheat oven to 375. Slice crab, reserving six pieces for garnish. Combine crab, rice, cheese, onions, tomatoes, chilies, salt, chili and garlic powders. Divide mixture among six individual buttered casseroles. Sprinkle with corn chips and garnish with reserved crab. Bake at 375 for 20 minutes, or until heated through and cheese is melted. Serves 6.

IV

SECOND BANANAS (Side Dishes)

In the 1960s, when my brand-new husband, Bob, was doing a pediatric residency program in Cleveland, he had supervision once a week with the famous baby doctor, Benjamin Spock. This was during Dr. Spock's highly visible activist days, and the demands on his time were endless.

So, week in and week out, what did Bob learn from the Master? "Each week I entered expectantly, sat in a chair and for sixty minutes watched Dr. Spock sip tea and field phone calls from all over the world. Not advising Queen Elizabeth to powder Prince Andrew's royal bottom, but instead words such as, 'Well, you tell Ho Chi Minh I am *not* a spokesman for the American public!'"

Although Dr. Spock did not consider himself a political spokesman, the parents of America would certainly be at a loss without his expert advice on prickly heat, pacifiers and Pablum.

And he obviously takes his own counsel because he still begins each day with — what else would a pediatrician eat for breakfast? — from-scratch oatmeal. Some things never change.

—L.A.

BENJAMIN SPOCK, M.D.

Physician, educator, author

Mother: Mildred (Stoughton) Spock

This is my favorite recipe. I cook and eat it every day for breakfast.

—Dr. Benjamin Spock

OATMEAL

½ cup steel-cut oats (not quick
    cooking oats)

2 cups water
dash of salt

Cook slowly over low heat for 30 minutes, stirring often. Serve with cream and maple syrup.

BILL ANDERSON

Country music singer, composer

Mother: Lib Anderson

My mother's father was a Methodist minister for most of his eighty-eight years on this earth, and I have many fond memories of mealtime at his house. Everybody knows Methodist ministers eat well!

On this particular occasion, however, my grandfather had traveled from Georgia to South Carolina to visit us — my mother, my father and me, his only grandson. The first morning he was with us, we gathered at the table for our morning meal and, as was his custom, Grandaddy took out his Bible and began reading aloud.

About five minutes into his devotional, I blurted out in all candor, "Grandaddy, *you* read the Bible at the breakfast table. My *daddy* reads the newspaper!"

The urge all these years to bounce a biscuit off my head notwithstanding, my mother has agreed to share with us two of her breakfast delights. (I was thinking of asking her for cornflakes with sliced bananas. She used to do that dish extremely well.)

—Bill Anderson

CHEESE SOUFFLÉ

3 tbl. margarine
3 tbl. flour
1 cup milk
1/2 tsp. salt

1 cup sharp Cheddar cheese,
grated
3 egg yolks
3 egg whites

Preheat oven to 350. Melt margarine. Add flour, stirring until smooth. Add milk and salt and continue stirring until mixture begins to thicken. Add cheese and continue stirring until thick. Add egg yolks, one at a time, mixing well. Beat egg whites until stiff. Fold into cheese mixture. Pour into soufflé dish which has been sprayed with Pam. Bake in preheated oven at 350 for 35 or 40 minutes.

CORNMEAL PANCAKES

1 1/2 cups cornmeal
1/2 cup flour
3/4 tsp. baking soda
3/4 tsp. salt

1 1/2 cups buttermilk
1 egg
1 tbl. molasses
2 tbl. melted shortening

Mix dry ingredients, add milk, beaten egg, molasses and melted shortening. Bake on hot griddle, using about 1/4 cup for each pancake.

JUDY WOODRUFF
Broadcast journalist

Mother: Anna Lee (Payne) Woodruff

When I was growing up we ate reasonably simple, healthy meals — chicken, steak, pork chops, potatoes and a lot of vegetables. My favorite meal was my mom's fried chicken, mashed potatoes and fresh green beans, all followed by her fabulous lemon meringue pie.

Also, I can't leave out her chocolate chip cookies — made with the Toll House recipe. These cookies are pure heaven!

Oh, I just remembered — her wonderful homemade dinner rolls — and even homemade bread, particularly when we lived in Taiwan as Army dependents. During that time, when she made fresh bread from scratch, she had to use ice cube trays. And she baked in a specially made tin oven, which she placed on our kerosene stove.

Mom also reminded me that her holiday dinners frequently went awry when we lived at various Army posts, because the oven would stop working in the midst of cooking a ham or turkey (usually for Christmas!).

Mother would not let us stay in the kitchen while she mixed up these rolls. While the rolls were baking, our mouths were watering as we smelled the delicious aroma.

—Judy Woodruff

ANNA LEE WOODRUFF'S REFRIGERATOR ROLLS

1 cup hot water	1 package dry yeast
1 tsp. salt	2 tbl. lukewarm water
6 tbl. shortening	1 egg
1/4 cup sugar	3 1/2-4 cups sifted all-purpose flour

Combine water, salt, shortening and sugar in large bowl. Stir until shortening is melted and salt and sugar dissolved. Cool to lukewarm or until a little of mixture dropped on inside of wrist feels almost cool. Meanwhile, sprinkle yeast in lukewarm water. Let stand 5-10 minutes until thoroughly dissolved. Stir well; then stir into shortening mixture. Beat egg well and add to shortening mixture. Next, add a cup of the flour. Beat well with spoon. Slowly stir in rest of flour — or enough to make dough easy to handle — not sticky. Grease top of dough with salad oil, stretching damp towel across dough. Then cover tightly with waxed paper or bowl cover, damp towel inside. Store in refrigerator. Use dough at once, or keep 2-3 days in refrigerator. Dampen towel as it dries. Punch down dough if it rises too close to top of bowl.

Preheat oven to 425. In using dough, cut off only as much as is needed, returning rest to refrigerator, covered. Shape into crescents or cloverleafs. Brush rolls with melted butter or margarine. Cover with towel. Let rise in warm place (80°-85°F) until double in bulk. When double in bulk, rolls will be so light you can hardly feel their weight when they are touched gently with your fingertip. Bake rolls in 425 oven for 12-15 minutes or until done. Remove rolls from oven, brush with salad oil, butter or margarine. Turn out on wire cake rack to cool. Yields about 18.

Sipping our coffees at a San Francisco diner, my husband, Warren, and I chatted with the waitress. We didn't notice the man enter until he swiveled his small frame down next to me and ordered "eleven fried eggs — sunny-side-up, a glass of ice water and no toast!"

Silently we watched him consume the dripping eggs, swallow the water, plunk down his money and leave.

As the waitress cleared his dishes, Warren marveled, "Wasn't that odd?"

"Yes," she replied, "it sure was. He usually orders a dozen."

—E.B.

HOYT AXTON

Country music singer, composer, actor

Mother: Mae (Boren) Axton

This recipe has been handed down through the generations of Axtons. I hope you like it. Happy Trails!

—**Hoyt Axton**

JALAPENO CORNBREAD

1½ cups cornmeal
3 tsp. baking powder
½ tsp. salt
1 cup sour cream
½ cup cooking oil
1 cup grated Cheddar cheese

3 eggs
1 cup cream-style corn
½ cup chopped jalapeño peppers (Ortega brand chilies for a milder taste)

Preheat oven to 350. Mix dry ingredients in bowl. Add remaining ingredients. Mix until moistened.

Pour into greased pie pan or 8″ x 8″ baking dish. Bake at 350° about 25 minutes or until lightly browned.

And this recipe came from my grandmother Boren to my mother, Mae.

—Hoyt Axton

GRANNY'S BUTTER ROLLS

1½ cups flour
½ tsp. salt
2 level tsp. baking powder
½ cup shortening
¾ cup milk

1¾ cups sugar
1½ sticks butter or margarine
(softened)
cinnamon

Preheat oven to 450. Sift flour, salt, and baking powder together. Add shortening and mix thoroughly. Add milk and mix until smooth. Take ½ the dough at a time and roll out on a floured board just as you would a pie crust. Take 1 stick softened butter or margarine and spread evenly over dough. Spread 1½ cups sugar evenly over buttered dough, then sprinkle liberally with cinnamon.

Roll up dough lengthwise, as you would a jellyroll, and cut in 1 or 2″ slices. Place cut side down at spaced intervals in buttered pan, brush lightly with remaining butter and sprinkle with remaining ¼ cup sugar.

Cook in 450 oven for 25 minutes. Serve hot with coffee or milk or serve as dessert topped with ice cream.

JUDITH IVEY

Actress, Tony Award Winner

Mother: Dorothy L. Ivey

I have made this bread to serve at Christmas since my daughter, Judy, was a teenager. It became a favorite of the family and a special touch to our holidays.

The first Christmas that Judy spent away from home was in 1979. She was appearing at the Arena Stage, Washington, D.C., in *Design For Living*. We arrived on December 1 to see the show, and I had one piece of luggage with a treat for her to open every day until December 25.

One of the early treats was a supply of my Orange Date Bread. I have also made the recipe for her agents and the cast of several of her shows, including *Hurly Burly*.

—Dorothy Ivey

ORANGE DATE BREAD

2 sticks butter (softened)
2 cups sugar
5 eggs
1 tbl. vanilla
1 (8-ounce) package chopped
  dates
1 pound orange slice candy
  (cut up)

2 cups pecans
1 (4-ounce) can coconut
4 cups sifted flour
½ tsp. baking soda
1 tsp. salt
¾ cup buttermilk

Preheat oven to 300. Cream butter and sugar until fluffy. Beat in eggs (one at a time) and add vanilla. Set aside. Mix chopped dates, candy, nuts and coconut with ½ cup of the designated flour. Add buttermilk, flour, baking soda and salt to first mixture. Fold in dates, etc., with first mixture. (This will be very thick.)

Grease and flour 3 small aluminum loaf pans. (A 10″ tube pan may also be used.) Spoon mixture into pans and bake in slow oven (about 300) until done. Remove from oven and add following glaze.

GLAZE

1 cup orange juice

2 cups sifted powdered sugar

Mix well and pour over hot cake. Cover cake and let stand in refrigerator before cutting. This bread can be kept for several days.

ERSKINE CALDWELL
Author and screenwriter

Mother: Caroline Preston (Bell) Caldwell

When Erskine and I were married in 1957, we each had special dishes that we liked to cook for Sunday dinner. Erskine's contribution was Black-Eyed Peas, cooked the way his mother had always done them, and I made a yellow cornbread from my mother's recipe to go with them.

As soon as Erskine had taught me exactly how to make Homestead Black-Eyed Peas, he happily retired from the kitchen and I made them as a weekly ritual.

During our thirty-year marriage, this was always Erskine's favorite dinner, and here are the recipes that kept him so happy.

—Virginia (Mrs. Erskine) Caldwell

HOMESTEAD BLACK-EYED PEAS

2 cans fresh shelled black-eyed
  peas
1 very large onion, chopped

1 cup diced, cooked ham
3 tbl. chopped parsley
salt and pepper to taste

Add ingredients to 2 cups water and simmer for 1½ hours or until liquid reaches consistency of thick soup. Stir often and add extra water if necessary. Serve with slices of hot cornbread. Serves 4.

MOTHER'S CORNBREAD

1 cup flour
¾ cup corn meal
¼ cup sugar
3 tsp. baking powder

½ tsp. salt
1 cup milk
1 egg beaten well
2 tbl. melted shortening

Preheat oven to 425. Combine and sift dry ingredients. Stir milk, egg and shortening until moist. Pour in buttered, floured cake pan. Bake for 20 minutes in 425 oven. Butter or margarine are best for shortening.

MARIO M. CUOMO

Governor of New York

Mother: Immaculata Cuomo

Polenta was the all-purpose meal in our house when I was growing up. My mother served it like farina for breakfast, or with chunks of meat or cheese at lunch and dinner. There was no question of our complaining about the sameness of our diet. We just did not have such a luxury in our house.

Polenta was our bread and potatoes, as well as our cereal. Through my mother, we recognized it as a staple of our survival. We therefore consumed it gratefully, and kept quiet.

—**Mario Cuomo**

POLENTA

1 13-ounce box "Fattorie & Pandea" instant Polenta (pre-cooked maize flour)

1½ quarts homemade (preferred) chicken stock

2 tsp. salt (optional)

olive oil

Bring chicken stock to a boil. Add polenta, reduce heat. Use long wooden spoon, stirring constantly. Cook approximately 5 minutes. Remove from heat. Spread mixture on baking sheet about ½″ thick. Refrigerate for 1½ hours. Cut polenta into squares or triangles. Fry in good quality olive oil until lightly browned on both sides. Serves 6.

AVNER EISENBERG

"Avner the Eccentric," Actor, New Vaudevillian

Mother: Mickie (Greenberg) Eisenberg

When Avner was a little boy, I became leader of his Cub Scout troop. One afternoon when I was driving four young Cubs home, we saw a teen-ager walking down the street with a live boa constrictor slung around his neck. Thinking, "This is educational," I stopped the car so Avner and his friends could examine the snake. Well, he flipped out and shortly thereafter formed a Snake Club.

He had his first snake when he was twelve years old, and our house became the least favorite run for the men on the UPS route. They delivered packages very gingerly, because most likely one of those sealed boxes would contain Avner's latest snake.

Avner's pride and joy, his boa, developed mites, so it needed a bath in grain alcohol. Since no store would sell grain alcohol to a twelve-year-old, I had to explain to the manager that it was for my son's snake. He didn't ask too many questions, but gave me that "Sure, lady!" look.

When we got home, Avner left his snake marinating in the bathtub. Later, when his father went to take a shower, he froze when he spied the snake coiled around the showerhead drunkenly peering down at him. Whispering "Excuse me," he high-tailed it out of the bathroom and invoked Avner's name with a yell which I'm sure Avner will never forget.

When Avner asked me to prepare his favorites, Fresh Artichokes or Lokshen Kugel, I was more than happy to comply. But, although I finally got used to his walking around the house with a live snake, I drew the line when it came to the force-feeding of little, live creatures to his pet in front of our dinner guests.

We had a happy, lively household. Avner enjoyed my cooking, and the boa thrived on his diet of baby chicks and mice.

Given a choice, I suspect you would prefer *my* recipes.

—**Mickie Eisenberg**

LOKSHEN KUGEL

1 pound medium noodles
3 large onions, chopped
1 12-oz. can mushroom stems and pieces

vegetable oil (approximately ¼ to ⅓ cup)
4 eggs, beaten well

Preheat oven to 350. Cook noodles according to package directions. Drain. Mix noodles with onions, mushrooms and beaten eggs. Add enough vegetable oil to hold mixture together. Spray 9″ x 13″ Pyrex pan with Pam. Bake in 350 oven for 1 hour or until brown. Serves 12.

DeFOREST KELLEY

(aka *Star Trek*'s Dr. McCoy), Actor

Mother: Clora Kelley

We ate lots of chicken when I was a youth in the South. My mother (since passed away) lost a diamond from her favorite ring while feeding her chickens one day. She later found it in the craw of a chicken she was preparing for dinner. Whenever I see a nude chicken, I always remember her joyful scream, announcing that she'd found her diamond. I wear that ring to this day.

—DeForest Kelley

COMPANY GRITS

4 cups water, salted	1 can cream of chicken soup,
1 cup grits	undiluted
1 cup grated Cheddar cheese	

Preheat oven to 325. Slowly add grits to boiling water. Simmer 5 minutes. Remove from heat. Fold in cheese and soup until completely blended. Pour into buttered casserole. Cover and bake in 325 oven for 30 minutes. Serves 8.

Aunt DeVera's mom and dad came over for lunch one day, and the main course was hamburger sandwiches. Her dad proceeded to load his bun with mustard, pickles, relish, ketchup and the works.

After several bites, he turned to his wife. "Lottie," he said, "why can't you cook like this? This is the best hamburger I've ever tasted, and it's really different."

Lottie looked down at his plate and snorted, "It should be different, you forgot to put your meat in the bun."

—E.B.

ALEX HALEY

Author, Pulitzer Prize winner

Mother: Bertha George (Palmer) Haley

Where would Mama's cooking be without the lessons handed down from Grandma?. . . .

My grandmother, Cynthia Murray Palmer, was of the "pinch-of-this, cup-of-that, dash-of-the-other" school. My favorite memory is that I used to sit in the sill of the kitchen window and lean my elbows on the table while my grandmother, on the opposite side, went about preparing things for cooking.

If something was edible, or almost so, such as teacake dough, she would frequently pop a bit of it into my mouth as we carried on conversations, punctuated by tidbits. It was across that table that Grandma told me many things about the family before us. That was where I heard so much about her grandfather, "Chicken

George," and her parents and others who would decades later appear in my book *Roots*.

As to specific dishes which I loved, I would say fried corn was one of my special favorites. Grandma's egg custard was another. Her fried chicken was, of course, like everybody else's grandmother's, classic. Her teacakes were warm and yellowish and crumbly, and I loved them more than real cakes.

You can get a little bit of an idea of what it was like in Grandma's kitchen in my boyhood home, which is now a museum in little Henning, Tennessee.

—**Alex Haley**

FRIED CORN

12 ears of fresh corn
½ stick butter
¼ cup bacon fat

3-4 tsp. sugar
salt and pepper

With sharp knife, scrape ears of corn with downward strokes. Melt butter in large skillet and add bacon fat. When hot, spoon in the corn and fry for 15 to 20 minutes — stirring continually. As corn cooks, add sugar. Salt and pepper to taste. Serves 6.

V

Encores

(Desserts)

LYNNE ALPERN

Author, lecturer

Mother: Ruth Shapiro

It was stormy that night of April 15. As usual my lawyer-dad, Julian, had finished his clients' tax returns early. All but his own. So he and Mother were making a last-minute run to the post office at 11:45 P.M.

At a red light on a heavily-trafficked street, Dad's Corvette refused to shift out of neutral. Nothing to do but call a wrecker. With cars whizzing by on both sides, Mother dodged traffic and made it to the nearest building, which she assumed was still a restaurant though operating under a different name.

Three men emerged and volunteered to push the car onto a side street out of harm's way. Then they invited Mother and Dad inside to use the phone, explaining that they were the night managers. Once inside, as my folks' eyes became accustomed to the dark interior, my seventy-eight-year-old dad and seventy-two-year-old mom saw cavorting onstage a girl wearing a blonde wig, red nail polish and a black G-string. Obviously this was no longer a restaurant.

The hospitable managers of the topless bar offered Dad their private telephone and brought them free drinks. And when their auto club couldn't provide equipment to handle a sports car in the middle of the night, the manager called his own wrecker. He then escorted my parents to the "Convention Room," where they could watch the floor show without being assaulted by high-decibel music.

The next day Mother decided to express her appreciation by baking the nightclub personnel a cheesecake, and she called the bartender to let him know of her impending arrival.

The cake was hot out of the oven when Mom walked in at 4:30 P.M. Much to her surprise, the floor show was already bumping and grinding along. The bartender, eagerly anticipating her gift, motioned her over, lifted the cover, sniffed the heavenly aroma and bellowed out, "Holy smokes, it's still hot!"

At that, twenty-three lusty Texans rose as one and clustered around Mom's cheesecake, leaving the half-nude stripper on stage to exhibit *her* wares to an empty house.

My mother, smiling philosophically, turned to the bartender and declared, "I could draw all sorts of conclusions from this, but I am content to realize that my cheesecake won out over hers . . . by a nose."

—L.A.

RUTH SHAPIRO'S LUSTY CHEESECAKE

5 eggs, room temperature	juice of 2 fresh lemons
1½ cups sugar	1 cup cream
1 tsp. vanilla	¼ cup flour
24 oz. cream cheese, room temperature	

111

CRUST

1 box vanilla wafers
1 tbl. sugar

1 tsp. cinnamon
1 stick melted butter

Do NOT preheat oven.

For crust: Crush vanilla wafers into fine crumbs in food processor. Or place wafers in plastic bag and crush with a rolling pin. Add sugar and cinnamon and mix well. Pour crumbs into 9″ x 13″ pan. Melt butter and slowly drizzle it over the crumbs (it is not necessary to stir crumbs). Set aside.

Filling: Separate eggs. In mixer beat egg yolks till light. Add sugar gradually and beat well. Add vanilla. Beat in cream cheese till well blended. Add lemon juice, cream, and flour. Beat well. In clean bowl, beat egg whites until stiff. Fold into cheese mixture and pour into crust.

Put in cold oven. Turn heat to 350. Bake 40 minutes. Turn oven off but don't open door. Let cheesecake stand in oven 20 minutes. Remove from oven and then get out of the way of the drooling crowd. Delicious warm or cold. Serves 16 at your house. At my house, 12 if I'm lucky.

Millions of people across the country begin their day with Willard Scott. But if Willard had his druthers, he'd start his day with a hefty slice of his favorite Brown Sugar Pound Cake. . . .

WILLARD SCOTT

TV weather reporter and performer

Mother: Thelma Matti (Phillips) Scott

BROWN SUGAR POUND CAKE

2 sticks butter
1/2 cup Crisco shortening
5 eggs
1 lb. and 1 cup light brown sugar

3 1/2 cups plain flour
1/2 tsp. baking powder
1 cup milk

Preheat oven to 325. Let eggs and butter "sit" till they're at room temperature. Cream together butter and Crisco. Add 5 eggs one at a time, creaming after each. Add brown sugar. Sift together flour and baking powder. Add flour mixture alternately with milk to sugar mixture. Bake at 325 in greased and floured tube pan for 1 1/4 to 1 1/2 hours.

FROSTING

1 stick butter
1 cup chopped pecans

1 box confectioner's sugar
milk to thin

Toast pecans in butter in thick broiler pan in the oven till they brown well. Let cool a little. In a bowl add confectioner's sugar to pecan mixture. Add milk enough to thin to spreading consistency. Spread on top of cake. Some should "drip" down sides and center but should not be spread anywhere except on top.

During WWII, butter was sometimes hard to come by, so the newspaper published dessert recipes substituting cooking oil instead.

My mother, expecting company for dinner, baked a beautiful cake for dessert, patriotically using cooking oil and gently stirring eight precious eggs into the unfamiliar terrain of oily batter, as had been prescribed.

With much fanfare, she proudly presented the delicately iced creation and, amidst "oohs" and "ahs," began to slice it open.

She removed the first piece. A startled guest blurted, "My God, Ruth, what have you done?" as Mother exposed, in the middle of the cake, a perfectly shaped hard-boiled egg.

Mumbling something about an old family tradition, Mom would not divulge the secret recipe to any of her guests. But I did hear her whisper to Dad disgustedly, "Tomorrow we buy a new stove."

—E.B.

JEFF VAN NOTE

Former professional football player, Atlanta Falcons

Mother: Gretchen Van Note

Mr. Van Note and I, who both had sons named Jeff, were married in 1963. But I had known the family since Big Jeff was six years old. My son, Little Jeff, and Big Jeff started first grade together.

For summers and holidays we had three sons and one daughter at home, and almost all the humorous incidents were played on our only daughter, Muff. She had quite a collection of dolls, and every evening the boys would hang one from the dining room chandelier. Thank God, she could certainly take a joke.

As to food, Big Jeff loved everything and anything chocolate, so here's his favorite cake recipe. It was also my favorite as it makes a large sheet cake and even with his football appetite will last more than an hour.

—Gretchen Van Note

SHEATH CAKE

2 cups flour
2 cups sugar
1 stick butter
1 cup water
4 tbl. cocoa
$^1/_2$ cup oil

2 eggs
$^1/_2$ cup buttermilk
1 tsp. baking soda
1 tsp. vanilla
1 tsp. cinnamon

Preheat oven 350. Sift and set aside flour and sugar. Bring to a boil butter, water, cocoa and oil. Beat slightly the eggs, buttermilk, soda, vanilla and cinnamon. Mix all together and pour into 16″ x 11″ pan. Bake at 350 20 to 25 minutes. Do not over-bake. Five minutes before cake is done, prepare icing.

ICING

1 stick butter
6 tbl. milk
4 tbl. cocoa

1 box confectioner's sugar
pecan pieces

Bring to boil butter, milk and cocoa. Pour over confectioner's sugar and mix well. Ice while cake is hot. Decorate with pecan pieces. Serves 24.

CHRISTOPHER PARKENING

Classical guitarist

Mother: Betty (Marshall) Parkening

Christopher's favorite, with many fond memories, is my mother's coffeecake, always known as "Grandmother's Coffeecake." Mother began baking this simple cake in the 1930s. Her kitchen would smell of cinnamon and spices when the children and I would come for a visit.

And when Mom came to our house, in no time at all my kitchen, too, would have the fragrance of those wonderful spices. (To this day, it is also my husband Duke's favorite cake.)

Chris and his sister, Terry, would look forward to warm coffeecake with butter in the morning or coffeecake with whipped cream and hot cocoa as dessert.

Today, Terry sees that Chris has "Grandmother's Coffeecake" at Christmas and New Year's and always on his birthday, since I now live in Idaho and they both live in Los Angeles.

Good memories are such a blessing, and it always makes me smile inside to know the children, who loved Mom dearly, still recall those lovely times of cake, cinnamon and spice.

—**Betty Parkening**

JESSIE LEE MARSHALL'S BUTTERMILK COFFEECAKE

1 cup sugar
1 stick melted butter
1 egg
2 cups flour
1 tsp. cinnamon
3/4 tsp. nutmeg

1 cup buttermilk
1/2 tsp. soda
1/4 tsp. salt
1 1/2 tsp. baking powder
nuts (optional)

Preheat oven to 350. Sift flour, add spices and sift again. Put soda in buttermilk. Cream butter, egg, sugar and salt together. Add sifted flour and buttermilk slowly.
Place in 9" x 9" pan. Cover with topping (add nuts if desired) and bake at 350 for 45 minutes.

TOPPING

1/2 cup brown sugar
3/4 tsp. cinnamon

nuts (optional)

Mix brown sugar and cinnamon together. Spread on batter before baking. Dot with butter and nuts (if desired). Serves 6-8.

JOSEPH PATERNO

Head coach, Penn St., *Sports Illustrated* '86 Sportsman of the Year

Mother: Florence (de LaSalle) Paterno

Joe Paterno's wife, Suzanne, scores points with the coach every time she passes him his favorite dessert.

PATERNO ORANGE CAKE

1 large Florida orange	2 large eggs
1 cup raisins	2 cups flour
1/3 cup walnuts	1 tsp. baking soda
1/2 cup vegetable shortening	1 tsp. salt
1 cup sugar	1 cup milk

Preheat oven to 350. Squeeze 1/3 cup juice from orange; reserve for Orange Nut Topping. Remove any seeds from orange.

Place unpeeled orange, raisins and nuts in blender or food processor. Process until finely ground. Set aside. In large mixer bowl, cream shortening and sugar; beat in eggs. Combine flour, baking soda and salt. Add to creamed mixture alternately with milk. Fold orange-raisin mixture into batter. Spread batter into a greased and floured 13" x 9" x 2" baking dish. Bake in a 350 oven 40 to 50 minutes. Cool 10 minutes.

ORANGE-NUT TOPPING

1/3 cup sugar	1 tsp. ground cinnamon
1/4 cup chopped walnuts	

Drizzle reserved 1/3 cup orange juice over warm cake. Combine sugar, walnuts and cinnamon; sprinkle over cake. Garnish with whole walnuts and orange slices, if desired. Makes 20 servings.

ED McMAHON

Television announcer and performer

Mother: Eleanor "Muth" McMahon

My mother made a delicacy called "radio doughnuts" that was a favorite of my father and me. Though they were called doughnuts, they looked nothing like a doughnut. They were just spoonfuls of batter dropped into hot oil. When cooked, no two looked alike. They were delicious!

She sprinkled some confectioner's sugar on them, and we couldn't wait until they cooled down enough to eat them. Years went by and no one ever asked her why they were called "radio doughnuts."

Then one day my curiosity peaked and I had to find out. I was awaiting some elaborate answer to the mystery, but all my mother said was, "Oh, I heard the recipe on the radio."

—Ed McMahon

RADIO DOUGHNUTS

4 beaten eggs	3 tsp. baking powder
²/₃ cup sugar	³/₄ tsp. salt
¹/₃ cup milk	1 tsp. cinnamon
¹/₃ cup shortening, melted	¹/₂ tsp. nutmeg
3¹/₂ cups sifted enriched flour	

Beat eggs and sugar 'til light; add milk and cooled shortening. Add sifted dry ingredients. Mix smooth. Drop small spoonfuls of dough into hot deep fat (375) until brown, turning once. Drain on paper towels. Be sure to fry at 375. If fat is too hot, doughnuts will be raw in the middle. If too cold, they will absorb too much fat. Optional: Sprinkle with granulated or powdered sugar after doughnuts are drained.

My mother grew up during the Depression, when she had to budget every penny. One day Mother's friend, Talli, called her excitedly. "Ruth, the drugstore is having a special on waffles. If we buy the first for twenty-five cents, the second one costs only a penny. How about it?" At thirteen cents a waffle, it sounded like a fine bargain to Mother, and off they went.

When the bill came, Talli, even poorer than Mother, picked up the check and split the tab. "I'm going to powder my nose, Ruth. Here's my share." When Mother looked down, there on the counter was Talli's shiny new penny.

It's been over fifty years, and I think by now it's high-time for Talli, now the celebrated Mrs. William Wyler, to fork over the twelve cents.

—L.A.

BOB DOLE

U.S. Senator from Kansas

Mother: Bina Dole

This cookie recipe has been a favorite of mine for many years, and I'm proud to say it is a favorite of my daughter, Robin, too. The taste of these cookies brings back many fond memories of times my daughter and I have spent together.

—**Bob Dole**

SEVEN-LAYER COOKIES

1 stick butter
1½ cups graham cracker crumbs
1 six ounce package chocolate
  chips
1 six ounce package
  butterscotch chips

1 small can shredded coconut
1 can Eagle Brand Sweetened
  Condensed Milk
1½ cups chopped pecans

Preheat oven to 350. Melt butter in 9″ x 11″ pan. Sprinkle cracker crumbs over melted butter. Sprinkle with chocolate chips, then butterscotch chips. Next, sprinkle coconut and add the chopped pecans on top. Pour Condensed Milk on top. DO NOT STIR. Bake for 30 minutes at 350. Cool and cut into 1½″ squares.

Sometimes, try as we might, the truth slips out. Such was the case at a potluck luncheon I recently attended. After the main course, my friend Jane proudly brought out a new dessert she had prepared for the first time called "Millionaire's Pie."

Eyeing the bumpy concoction warily and unable to turn her down completely, I sang out, "Give me a nickel's worth, please."

—L.A.

WALLY AMOS

"Cookie King," winner of the 1987 Horatio Alger Award.

Mother: Ruby Amos

For most children learning to cook, the first recipe they try is the universally loved chocolate chip cookie. And because so many mothers served these warm, melty-goodness morsels as treats when we were very young, each of us has our own special memories tied up in these culinary wonders.

Famous Amos has surely found a way to stir in those memories along with the chocolate chips — cookies with a heart. The next time you want to create something memorable for your family, try this Famous Amos variation on a classic. . . .

Encourage your cookies as they bake. Talk to them and watch them closely. It might be necessary to turn the tray around if your oven bakes unevenly. Give your cookies love and they'll grow up to be very pretty and tasty. Good luck, and have a very brown day.

—Famous Amos

125

FAMOUS AMOS'S RAISIN-FILLED CHOCOLATE CHIP COOKIES

2 sticks margarine, softened
3/4 cup firmly packed light brown sugar
3/4 cup granulated sugar
1 tsp. vanilla
1 tsp. water
2 medium-sized eggs

2 1/2 cups sifted, all-purpose flour
1 tsp. baking soda
1/2 tsp. salt
2 cups raisins
1 pkg. (12 oz.) semisweet chocolate pieces

Preheat oven to 375. Beat softened margarine, brown and white sugars in a large bowl with electric mixer until creamy. Add vanilla, water and eggs and blend thoroughly. By hand stir in flour, baking soda and salt until well mixed. Stir in raisins and chocolate pieces.

Using teaspoon from measuring set, spoon dough by teaspoonfuls onto cookie sheets. Allow 1 to 1 1/2 inches between cookies for spreading. Bake in moderate oven (375) for 8 minutes, or until cookies are nicely browned . . . depending on how crisp or well-done you like them. Makes about 6 dozen.

From a sweet melody on the stage to a winsome medley in the kitchen, Sheila MacRae always makes beautiful music for her famous offspring. . . .

MEREDITH MacRAE

Actress

Mother: Sheila MacRae

CRÈME BRULÉE

2 cups half-and-half
2 cups heavy cream
8 egg yolks (whites can be
frozen for another recipe)

½ cup granulated sugar
2 tsp. vanilla extract
1 cup dark brown sugar
Fresh fruit (optional)

Preheat oven to 350. This dessert is baked in a shallow 6-cup Pyrex dish, ceramic pan or soufflé dish placed in a larger pan filled with hot water.

In a saucepan, heat the half-and-half and cream slowly, stirring until hot. Do not scald or boil. Set aside. Beat egg yolks in the baking dish with a wire whisk, adding

127

granulated sugar gradually until the mixture is light-colored and creamy. Add a little of the hot cream to the yolks to warm them and stir quickly to blend. Add the rest of the hot cream and the vanilla, mixing well. Cover the dish with foil and set into a pan of hot water. Bake at 350 for about 1 hour and 15 minutes, or until the custard is set. To test, insert a knife ½ inch from the center. It should come out clean. Remove from the oven and from the pan of water. Chill thoroughly.

Using a large-mesh kitchen strainer, sprinkle brown sugar evenly over the top of the chilled custard. Set the dish in a bed of ice and place the custard under a *hot* broiler about 4 inches from the heat for 3 or 4 minutes, watching it carefully so that the sugar bubbles but doesn't burn. Serve immediately or refrigerate, uncovered, until serving time. Serve the custard plain or spoon it over fresh fruit. Serves 8.

To make ahead: This dessert may be made a day or two ahead and chilled. Do not glaze with brown sugar until the morning you plan to serve it, because the topping will turn to liquid if left longer. It will still be delicious that way but will turn into a Crème Caramel.

ORRIN G. HATCH

U.S. Senator from Utah

Mother: Helen (Kamm) Hatch

CHIPPED CHOCOLATE PIE

35 large marshmallows
½ cup milk
2 squares chipped bitter or
unsweetened chocolate

½ pint whipped whipping cream
or 1 small container of Cool Whip
graham cracker crust
chopped nuts, cherries, or chipped
sweetened chocolate for garnish

Melt marshmallows with milk in double boiler or microwave. Cool. Beat well. Fold in chipped bitter or unsweetened chocolate and whipping cream (or Cool Whip). Pour into graham cracker crust. Top with chopped nuts, cherries, or chipped chocolate — as desired. Chill in refrigerator for at least 2 hours.

PORTER WAGONER

Country music singer and composer

Mother: Bertha Wagoner

My mother taught me this recipe when I was a boy and I've never forgotten it.

—Porter Wagoner

PORTER WAGONER FUDGE

2 cups sugar
2 heaping tbl. cocoa
1/2 tsp. salt
1/4 cup Log Cabin syrup
milk

2 tbl. butter
1 tsp. vanilla
2 tbl. peanut butter
1/2 cup English walnuts

Mix sugar, cocoa, salt and syrup in saucepan. Add enough milk to make it soupy, but very thick. Bring to boil and boil until sugar is dissolved (4-5 minutes).

Test by dropping a spoonful into a cup of cold water until it forms a soft ball. Remove from heat and add butter and vanilla. Stir until it begins to cool. Add peanut butter and walnuts. Pour into large platter until it cools and hold a gun on yourself until you taste it!

LAURENCE J. PETER
Educator, author

Mother: Vicenta (Stevens) Peter

During the Great Depression, and frankly it wasn't that great, my mother, sister and I lived in a small primitive house in a municipality near the city of Vancouver, British Columbia, Canada. We were very poor, so my mother raised a big vegetable garden which provided us with most of our food.

When we could afford it, she bought a pot roast. She browned it and then cooked it slowly for a long time. This along with fresh vegetables, corn, potatoes, green beans, squash and tomatoes, from the garden constituted some of the most delectable and memorable meals of my childhood.

My mother was a gentle, kind woman with infinite patience. She became a gardener through necessity and developed into an expert horticulturist, honored by the Royal Horticulturist Society and awarded trophies for her development of new varieties of tuberous begonias and for the quality of her vegetables.

One of my favorite desserts was her rice pudding, which I've never seen duplicated elsewhere. Mother made it in a large flat pan in the oven. She put long grain brown rice, milk and muscat raisins in the pan and stirred it every time a skin developed on the top. The result was a golden-colored, creamy, caramel-flavored pudding.

—**Laurence Peter**

SAVORY RICE PUDDING

4 cups milk	1 tsp. vanilla
1/2 cup brown rice	3 tbl. melted butter
1/2 cup molasses	2 eggs, well beaten
pinch of salt	1/2 cup raisins

Preheat oven to 250. Mix the milk with well beaten eggs. Add rice, molasses, salt, raisins and vanilla and pour into greased baking dish. Bake at 250 for 3 hours, stirring several times during the first hour. Add the butter the last time you stir your pudding. Serves 4-6.

NANCY WILSON
Singer

Mother: Bertha Wilson

I put Jello in it once and that was enough for Nancy. She does not like Jello in her Trifle!

—Bertha Wilson

TRIFLE

1 box lemon cake mix
2 boxes instant lemon pudding
4 cups milk

2 boxes frozen strawberries
1 large Cool Whip
1 box strawberry Jello (optional)

Make two-layer cake with cake mix. Cool. Mix lemon pudding with milk according to directions on box. Alternate cake, pudding, strawberries and Cool Whip in a large bowl or individual dishes. If Jello is used, include it in layering.

BETTY TALMADGE

Businesswoman, party planner, caterer, former Washington hostess

Mother: Stella Shingler

My mother and grandmother were excellent Southern cooks. But when I wanted to help, Mother said, "Get out of the way, you make too much of a mess." I have memories of both of them cooking over a wood-burning stove. I'll never forget that smell!

We had Southern staples, though my mother did try to cut down on fat and calories. Father was a doctor and had diabetes, so she was a bit ahead of her time as far as knowledge of nutrition.

Back in my growing-up days, the dinner was at midday. Leftovers were covered and left out on the table for supper. During the week we didn't follow a set menu, but Sunday dinner was always fried chicken, stewed corn, fresh vegetables and cornbread. There's a secret to great cornbread . . . it's in the way you bake it. I put it under the broiler for a few minutes.

Mother also served turnip greens, and we always had to drink the "pot likker," hot from a cup, like soup, " 'cause that's where all the vitamins are."

After I married, Mother came to dinner. She was always a good guest, grateful for someone else to cook (particularly this time-consuming delectable Charlotte Russe, which was handed down from my mother and grandmother).

—Betty Talmadge

CHARLOTTE RUSSE

$1/2$ tbl. gelatin
$1/4$ cup cold milk
$1/4$ cup warm milk
1 pint whipping cream
1 tsp. vanilla

$1/2$ cup sugar
sherry
5 egg whites, beaten stiff
ladyfingers, split

Soften gelatin in cold milk. Dissolve in warm milk. Whip cream until stiff. Add vanilla, sugar, and sherry to taste. Add gelatin. Fold in egg whites. Pour into bowl or dessert glasses lined with ladyfingers. Serves 6.

CATHY LEE CROSBY

Actress

Mother: Linda (Hayes) Crosby

My mom always made this for my birthday. It is all I ever asked for. She has even made it and frozen it to send to me wherever I may be appearing. I have even hopped a flight to Palm Springs to get some. It is that good!

—Cathy Lee Crosby

137

PERSIMMON PUDDING
(Serve With Hard Sauce)

1¼ cup persimmon
1 cup sugar
1 cup flour
½ cup sweet milk
1 egg, well beaten

2 tbl. butter
½ tsp. salt
½ tsp. cinnamon
2 tsp. baking soda

Preheat oven to 350. Cream butter and sugar. Add well-beaten egg and persimmon pulp. Mix soda, salt, cinnamon and flour. Add to butter mixture, alternating with milk. Bake in covered dish at 350 for 45 minutes or until toothpick comes out clean when stuck in center.

HARD SAUCE

1 stick butter
1 cup powdered sugar

2 tsp. rum
vanilla

Cream butter with powdered sugar — a little at a time. Blend well. Then add rum. Add vanilla to taste. Chill. Serves 4.

VI

CRITICS' CORNER

Although good cooking and warm memories are an unbeatable combination, they don't necessarily go hand in hand. Several celebrities wrote us that their mothers, as **Lee Remick** remarked, "never went near a kitchen." Even **Julia Child**, the queen of cuisine, confided that her mother didn't spend much time in the kitchen and the famous "French Chef" didn't become interested in food until after she married. So if cooking wasn't your mother's forte, take heart — you are in good company.

While stars may occasionally kid their mothers about their kitchen foibles, professional comedians regularly find abundant fodder in Mama's culinary fiascos. **Buddy Hackett**, for instance, says that when his mother, Anna Hacker, fed him, he always thought heartburn was a natural consequence of eating. "So when I joined the Army, I thought I was dying when the fire went out."

And **Robin Williams** tells about one Thanksgiving when his mother, Laurie, made a turkey but forgot to remove the plastic bag of giblets. "I called that bird the 'toxic avenger turkey.' When Mom served it, she asked, 'You want dark meat, white meat or plastic dip?'"

Obviously, whether these prominent people ate their green beans or not, it hasn't seemed to diminish their success. And if "you are what you eat," their mothers must have dished up *something* right. We suspect it was lots of love, caring and the ability to laugh at their mistakes.

Perhaps that's where their children learned that it's OK occasionally to bite the hand that feeds you. Take Cookie's family. When our friend vacations with her family and they drive past a roadside restaurant touting "Home Cooking," Cookie's children beg, "Oh, Dad, please don't stop!"

DOUGLAS FAIRBANKS, JR.

Actor, producer, writer, winner of countless awards

Mother: Beth (Sully) Fairbanks

I was so flattered to be invited to submit a memory of my mother's cooking for your book. Unfortunately, my mother's only talent for cooking stopped at preparing toast in the toaster!

—**Douglas Fairbanks, Jr.**

HELEN GURLEY BROWN

Author, editor of *Cosmopolitan*

Mother: Cleo (Sisco) Gurley

My mother couldn't cook worth a damn and I wouldn't give *anyone* a recipe of hers! The few times that we had company, it was trauma city. She did make pretty good waffles, but I think mine are better and anyway I don't have her waffle recipe. She was a great mother otherwise.

—Helen Gurley Brown

It's one thing for mothers to cook for their famous offspring. But what happens when a celebrity spreads his wings and temporarily comes to rest in *your* roost? Ah, that's enough to ruffle anyone's feathers. . . .

Although I grew up knowing that Aaron Copland was my cousin, our paths never crossed until I went to graduate school in Cleveland, Ohio, in 1966.

Hearing that he would be guest conducting at the Cleveland Symphony Orchestra, where I ushered every week, and knowing he was fond of family, I got up my nerve and wrote him. We agreed on a Saturday lunch at my apartment, the only free time on his schedule.

The week arrived, and I excitedly attended a rehearsal (a truly boring experience, I discovered, for any but the most devoted student of music). When I went backstage afterwards to meet him in person, I was horrified to see this Pulitzer Prize-winning composer dining on the Frankenstein of mutant food, a vending machine sandwich. Aaron greeted me warmly and, with a twinkle in his eye, waved his limp cheese sandwich in my direction. "Now," he said, "you know the secret of my inspiration."

Our celebration lunch on Saturday, with my brother and a few friends, was a delight from beginning to end, with Aaron regaling us with tales of his travels both here and abroad. He also gratefully devoured the meal, which featured "Jake's Fish a la Veracruzana."

I don't know if there's any truth to the rumor that fish is "brain" food, but I do know that only twelve short months after eating that lunchtime repast, Aaron Copland composed *Inscape*. So pass the snapper, Louise!

—**LA**

JAKE'S FISH À LA VERACRUZANA

2 lbs. fish fillets
3 tomatoes
2 onions
12 pitted black olives
1 clove garlic
1 tbl. capers
1 green pepper

4 tbl. vinegar
1/2 cup olive oil
1 cup white wine
salt
pepper
oregano
parsley

This dish is highly flexible and can be varied by each cook, according to taste.

First, prepare your vegetables: peel and cut tomatoes in hunks, seed and cut peppers into strips, and slice onions and olives. Then in a heavy saucepan which has a lid, pour the olive oil. Add onions, tomatoes, olives, peppers, capers, garlic and 1/2 cup white wine.

Cook until this reduces a little, say 5 minutes. Now add your fish, salt, pepper, a sprig of parsley, one teaspoon dried or a sprig of fresh oregano, and wet down with the other 1/2 cup of wine. Cover and simmer 5-10 minutes, depending on thickness of fish. When cooked through, fish will flake easily with a fork. Serve over white or yellow rice. Serves 6-8.

When it comes to feeding celebrities, you'd think professional restaurateurs would have an edge over us "amateurs." And yet even they sometimes find themselves in a stew. . . .

Walk into Frenchman Camille Berman's restaurant, Maxim's in Houston, and on any particular day you might bump into actress Gene Tierney, the CEO of Kaiser Steel, the son of the President of Mexico, or even Joe Namath. A fixture in Houston society for over thirty years, Maxim's was the choice for Lyndon Johnson's fiftieth birthday celebration and is still the hangout for countless "Tall Texans."

One night **Johnny Carson** was in town and came for dinner. A nervous busboy dropped a whole tray of dirty dishes down his neck. Says Berman, in his charming Gallic accent, "Carson was a perfect gentleman. He stood up, bowed, took off his jacket and handed it to the busboy. 'Here, keep this as a souvenir!'"

If coping with famous customers is not enough challenge, Berman has also had to learn to adapt his French customs to the flamboyant antics of died-in-the-wool Texans. One night **Bob Kleeberg** (of the King Ranch) wanted Café Brulot, a flaming dessert coffee. Berman himself fixed it tableside with savoir-faire, using only the finest ingredients.

After Berman finished all that meticulous, expensive work, Kleeberg threw it into the ice bucket and said, "Now, Frenchie, I'll show you how we make it in Texas!" With that he whacked an orange into four pieces, threw it in the pan, poured Old Taylor bourbon over it, set it on fire and doused it with coffee.

Then there was the time McIntyre, the rancher, ordered turtle soup. Berman apologized: no turtles available. Later that afternoon McIntyre phoned Berman.

"Camille, there's a turtle waiting for you across the street in the garage." Sure enough, McIntyre had gone out and unearthed — as only millionaires can — a five-hundred-pound turtle, glued a broom handle to its hefty shell and chained it to a post in the parking garage!

Berman was speechless but not completely surprised. After all, McIntyre was also the man who, not finding watermelon on the menu, had an entire truckful of the juicy fruits unloaded on a busy downtown street, smack dab in front of the restaurant. "Now may I have some watermelon?" he asked innocently. Some things they don't teach you at the Cordon Bleu.

Phyllis Diller says, "Be good to your children. Remember, they're going to pick out the nursing home." So, like the other mothers in this book, we have done our share of coddling, chopping, mixing and fixing to create gastronomic subliminal messages which we hope will trigger fond reminiscences now and guilty gratitude in the future.

Thus, we thought, it would be enchanting to ask our own offspring the same question we asked our celebrities: "What is your favorite recipe and mealtime memory of Mom?" And this is the thanks we get. . . . (first from Esther)

When I asked my son, Josh, which of my recipes should be included in this book, he stared at me vacantly. Confiscating his car keys, I pressed on. "Just tell me which meal — out of the many I've prepared for you, so lovingly with my own hands these past twenty years — is your favorite?" Hunkering down in his chair, he thought awhile and then brightened. "I've got it, Mom, I love your TV dinners!"

Here, then, is his second choice, my "Chicken with Sherry Wine Sauce." But remember, this preference is from a college student whose main nourishment for nine months out of the year comes from the Four Basic Junk Food Groups: Chips, Twinkies, Coca-Cola and Moon Pies.

CHICKEN WITH SHERRY WINE SAUCE

8 boned chicken breasts
1 cup flour
1 tsp. Lawry's Seasoned Salt
1 stick butter or margarine
8 oz. fresh mushrooms

2 small onions, chopped fine
1 cup sherry wine
2 cans Campbell's Beef Broth
2 tbl. ketchup
2 tbl. cornstarch

Preheat oven to 350. Mix flour with Lawry's Seasoned Salt. Dredge chicken breasts in flour to coat. Brown chicken in butter or margarine until golden on both sides. Remove chicken and place pieces side by side in baking dish. Do not overlap chicken. Set aside.

Sauté onions in same pan you used for the chicken. If you have to add a little butter, do so. When onion is soft, add mushrooms and continue to sauté 5 minutes more. Add sherry. Simmer together over low heat.

While this cooks, in another bowl mix soup, ketchup and cornstarch. Blend together and add to simmering wine sauce. Simmer for 5 minutes more or until well blended. Pour over the chicken. Sauce will not be thick but will cook into the chicken while it bakes. Bake in 350 oven about one hour. Baste every 15 minutes. This dish freezes well. (Thaw in refrigerator. Reheat for one hour and serve). Serves 6.

In my own defense, I realize now that perhaps my culinary skills peaked too soon. Let me explain. . . .

Andy Warhol said that everyone, once in his lifetime, would be famous for fifteen minutes. I, of course, owe my fifteen minutes in the sun to the Chinese, my mother-in-law, Fannie and the *Chicago Tribune.*

Before Josh was born, the *Tribune* ran a contest for the best recipe of the week. The winner received five dollars, and the paper published both the recipe and a photo of the winning cook. I decided to submit Mom's recipe for Chinese Pepper Steak, which Warren relished (until I cooked it so often that he begged me to stop).

Now, I don't know where Mom got the recipe, and I know it sure wasn't an old kosher family specialty. But it did win the prize, and the editor requested that I come downtown to have my picture taken.

Nothing in my closet was conservative enough to wear to the *Tribune* offices. I was, after all, a subscriber of the more liberal *Chicago Sun-Times.* Thus I went shopping for a new outfit and had my hair done for the occasion. That night Warren thoughtfully invited me out for dinner to celebrate my culinary victory.

All in all, between the dress, my hair and dinner, my winning entry cost $179.25, minus my five dollar prize ($4.23 after the IRS took its share). I guess that's what they mean by the price of fame. Thanks a lot, Andy. Most of us can't afford more than fifteen minutes . . . at least in this lifetime.

CHINESE PEPPER STEAK

1 lb. sirloin steak
1/4 cup soy sauce
1 tsp. sugar
2 large tomatoes
1/2 tsp. ginger
2 large green peppers

1/4 cup olive oil
1 clove garlic, sliced fine
2 tbl. cornstarch
1 tsp. soy sauce
1/4 cup water

Slice beef into very thin strips. Pour 1/4 cup soy sauce and sugar over meat and marinate for 30 minutes. Meanwhile cut green peppers and tomatoes into 1" cubes. Heat oil in skillet and add garlic and ginger. After one minute, remove garlic. Add meat and its liquid and sauté for 6 minutes.

Add tomatoes and green peppers and sauté for 3 minutes. Mix cornstarch with water and a teaspoon of soy sauce. Add to mixture and gently stir for another minute. Entire cooking period takes 10 minutes over medium heat. Serve with rice and Chinese noodles. Serves 4.

And how do you suppose Lynne fared with *her* children? Here's a word from her son, Ken, and daughter, Eve:

"We thought this book was supposed to be a comedy, not a horror story! However, the *Texas Chainsaw Massacre* paled in comparison when our mom, normally a terrific cook, went on a health food kick. Nothing serious, just a little sprout-and-tofu madness.

"She began experimenting with all kinds of tofu dishes — Oriental stir fry, casseroles, even (if you can imagine) green tofu mayonnaise. Some weren't . . . inedible. Nevertheless, we both complained and groaned with each new 'treat.' We began eyeing with suspicion any dish whose every ingredient was not immediately recognizable.

"So Mom switched into her 'covert' mode. Our family watchword became, 'OK, where did Mom hide the tofu tonight?' Some dishes, like Tofu Lasagna, still slipped by us unsuspected. But the Tofu Pie took the cake. It sported a graham cracker crust with a gooey-sweet filling made of tofu, carob powder (a chocolate substitute which looks like cocoa and tastes like nothing) and honey.

"We all took an exploratory bite, which was one too many, and in vain tried to think of one nice thing to say about it. Even Dad, who loves food and has consumed regional specialties from China to Morocco without inflicting permanent damage, couldn't get past that first mouthful.

"Come to think about it, there *is* one good thing to say about Tofu Pie after all: it cured Mom once and for all of her tofu mania. Now, when Mom cooks, it's always *real* food, and for special occasions we always request our all-time favorite, Moroccan

Lamb. Try it sometime when you have a free afternoon, and be sure to make the pepper salad and oranges that go with it. We can testify that it's fantastic, tofu-free, and worth the work (especially if your mom does it *for* you). The best part is, to be authentic, you're supposed to eat the entire meal with your fingers. Bon appetit!"

MOROCCAN LAMB

6-7 lb. leg of lamb
3½ tsp. ground coriander seed
3 cloves garlic, peeled and mashed

1½ tsp. ground cumin
¾ tsp. paprika
5 tbl. unsalted butter
salt

Remove excess fat from leg of lamb. In food processor, using a mortar & pestle, or by hand, blend all ingredients except lamb into a paste. With a sharp knife make several deep gashes in the meat and stuff with small amounts of the paste. Rub remaining paste over the lamb. Let stand one hour.

Preheat oven to 475. Place on the middle shelf of the oven and roast 20 minutes. Reduce the heat to 350 and continue roasting for about 2½ hours, or until the meat can easily be separated from the bone with a fork. Baste every 15 minutes with the pan juices. (This is the secret to having a crispy brown crust, while keeping the meat inside juicy and tender.) Serve very hot.

The traditional serving style is for guests to eat with their fingers, removing chunks of meat directly from the bone. I've never once had a guest ask for a fork — it's too much fun. Serve with pita bread, green pepper and tomato salad, and orange slices, for a delectable contrast of tastes and textures. Serves 8.

GREEN PEPPER AND TOMATO SALAD

4 green peppers
5 large ripe tomatoes, peeled,
   seeded and chopped
1/3 cup olive oil
2 garlic cloves, crushed
juice of 1 lemon

1 tsp. cumin
1/4 tsp. paprika
1/8 tsp. cayenne pepper
salt and freshly ground pepper

Grill peppers over direct flame on gas stove top or under broiler until charred (I've even done it over candles). Remove skin and seeds and cut peppers into short strips. Combine with remaining ingredients, mixing well. Cover and chill. Serves 8.

ORANGE SLICES

6 navel oranges, peeled and
   sliced into rounds
2 tbl. powdered sugar

1 tsp. rose water or orange
   flower water
1/4-1/2 tsp. cinnamon

Arrange orange slices in overlapping pattern in serving dish. Sprinkle with remaining ingredients, cover and chill before serving. Serves 8.

So, Mama, what *do* you feed a celebrity? Well, whether you're a four-star chef or just beginning your culinary adventures, the secret is to treat your family like celebrities and visiting celebrities like family. Then, in case Charles and Di drop in for a bite, they'll leave with delicious memories.

But remember, you're only the cook. When it comes to digesting, they're on their own.

Kathryn Heath Gable

Esther Blumenfeld and Lynne Alpern are free-lance journalists and the authors of two books, *Oh, Lord, I Sound Just Like Mama* and *The Smile Connection.* They conduct seminars nationwide on writing and humor. In 1987 the Dixie Council of Authors and Journalists named them Georgia Authors of the Year in the humor category.